San Mateo de Cangrejos

SUNY series, Afro-Latinx Futures

———————

Vanessa K. Valdés, editor

San Mateo de Cangrejos

HISTORICAL NOTES ON A SELF-EMANCIPATED BLACK COMMUNITY IN PUERTO RICO

Gilberto Aponte Torres

TRANSLATED BY
KAREN JUANITA CARRILLO

FOREWORD TO THE TRANSLATION BY
VANESSA K. VALDÉS

Cover: *A peon cabin, San Turce, Porto Rico.* ca. 1900. Photograph. Library of Congress.

Published by State University of New York Press, Albany

© 2023 State University of New York

All rights reserved

Printed in the United States of America

No part of this book may be used or reproduced in any manner whatsoever without written permission. No part of this book may be stored in a retrieval system or transmitted in any form or by any means including electronic, electrostatic, magnetic tape, mechanical, photocopying, recording, or otherwise without the prior permission in writing of the publisher.

For information, contact State University of New York Press, Albany, NY
www.sunypress.edu

Library of Congress Cataloging-in-Publication Data

Names: Aponte Torres, Gilberto, 1956– author. | Carrillo, Karen Juanita, translator.
Title: San Mateo de Cangrejos : historical notes on a self-emancipated Black community in Puerto Rico / Gilberto Aponte Torres ; translated by Karen Juanita Carillo.
Other titles: San Mateo de Cangrejos. English | Historical notes on a self-emancipated Black community in Puerto Rico
Description: Albany : State University of New York Press, [2023]. | Series: SUNY series, Afro-Latinx futures | Translation of: San Mateo de Cangrejos, comunidad cimarrona en Puerto Rico: notas para su historia. | Includes bibliographical references and index.
Identifiers: LCCN 2022021024 | ISBN 9781438491516 (hardcover : alk. paper) | ISBN 9781438491530 (ebook)
Subjects: LCSH: Maroons—Puerto Rico—San Juan—History. | Africans—Puerto Rico—San Juan—History. | Santurce (San Juan, P.R.)—History. | Santurce (San Juan, P.R.)—Race relations—History. | San Juan (P.R.)—Race relations—History. | Puerto Rico—Race relations—History. | San Juan (P.R.)—History.
Classification: LCC F1981.S2 A74 2023 | DDC 972.95/00496—dc23/eng/20220504
LC record available at https://lccn.loc.gov/2022021024

10 9 8 7 6 5 4 3 2 1

Gilberto Aponte Torres

To all the Black Puerto Ricans who will find that in their past they had dignity and a national conscience.

To Confesor Aponte, a man of the Black race who was my father's father.

Karen Juanita Carrillo

To the Afro Puerto Ricans who are challenging and reshaping Puerto Rico's understanding of its ethnic identity.

To my father, Manuel Roland Carrillo Sr., and grandfather, Teodoro Carrillo Cardona.

Contents

List of Illustrations	ix
Translator's Note	xi
Foreword to the Translation	xv
Vanessa K. Valdés	
Prologue to Original	xvii
Acknowledgments	xix
Abbreviations	xxi
Introduction	1
Chapter 1 San Mateo de Cangrejos's Origins	3
Chapter 2 The Church of Cangrejos	9
Chapter 3 Economic Activity in Cangrejos in the Eighteenth and Nineteenth Centuries	11
Chapter 4 Ethnic Origins of San Mateo de Cangrejos	23
Chapter 5 San Mateo de Cangrejos and Military Defense	25

viii | Contents

Chapter 6	The Suppression of Cangrejos in 1862	27
Chapter 7	The Institutional Order of Cangrejos	33
Chapter 8	Cangrejos's Residents: As Seen from San Juan	37
Chapter 9	Santurce's Urban and Demographic Development	41
Conclusion		45
Appendix		47
Glossary		57
Notes		59
Bibliographies		65
Index		67

Illustrations

Figures

1.1	Porto-Rico.	5
1.2	Porto-Rico with Cangrejos focus.	6
2.1	Church of San Mateo de Cangrejos.	10
6.1	Train bridge over the Martin Peña channel, San Juan, Puerto Rico.	30
8.1	Detail of towers and rear of pediment from roof.	40
8.2	Detail bell tower, southwest corner.	40

Tables

3.1a	Leases of passages and river estuaries, 1761, 1765, and 1819.	13
3.1b	Total value table.	15
3.2	Value and relative importance of agrofishing production in Cangrejos, 1818.	16
3.3	Number of heads of households in Cangrejos, 1820–1866.	17
3.4	Municipal income for public expenditures in Cangrejos, 1820–1832.	17

x | List of Illustrations

3.5 Subsidy payments in Cangrejos, by neighborhood, 1825–1832.   18

3.6 Cultivated lands and their estimated value in Cangrejos, 1842.   18

3.7 Animals reported in Cangrejos in 1842.   19

3.8 Wealth in Cangrejos in 1862.   20

3.9 Sources of wealth in Cangrejos, 1862.   20

3.10 Land tenure in the parts of Cangrejos annexed to San Juan, 1864.   21

A.1 Origin of the baptized in San Mateo de Cangrejos, 1773–1900.   47–48

A.2 Deaths in Cangrejos, 1854–1900.   48

A.3 Population of San Mateo de Cangrejos, 1765–1861.   49

A.4 Ethnic composition of San Mateo de Cangrejos, 1765–1861.   50–53

A.5 Population structure by age in San Mateo de Cangrejos, 1765 and 1841.   54

A.6 Known authorities in Cangrejos between 1773 and 1876.   55

A.7 Important dates and events in San Mateo de Cangrejos.   56

Translator's Note

This book was originally written as part of a celebration of the many towns and cities that make up Puerto Rico by one of the island's oldest banks, Banco Popular (a financial institution founded in 1893, just five years before Puerto Rico was annexed by the United States of America).[1] *San Mateo de Cangrejos, comunidad cimarrona en Puerto Rico: Notas para su historia* was one of a series of books written for the Banco Popular celebration—and, in fact, this book became a bestseller in the series. Other books in the series include *Villalba: Notas para su historia: (estampas de Villalba ayer y hoy)* by Jorge de la Cruz Figueroa; *Vega Baja: Notas para su historia* by Luis de la Rosa Martínez; *Guayanilla, notas para su historia* by Otto Sievens Irizarry; *Cabo Rojo: Notas para su historia* by Antonio Ramos y Ramírez de Arellano; *Mayagüez: Notas para su historia* by Silvia Aguiló Ramos; and *Fajardo: Notas para su historia* by Nilsa Rivera Colón.

I was interested in translating *San Mateo de Cangrejos, comunidad cimarrona en Puerto Rico: Notas para su historia* because of its subject matter. *San Mateo de Cangrejos, comunidad cimarrona en Puerto Rico* is the story of the founding of an area that is today known as Santurce, a district that is part of the city of San Juan. With 40 "subbarrios" or subdistricts, Santurce today boasts some of the island's wealthiest districts—including Miramar, Ocean Park, and Condado.

Today's resort-filled, stylish, and art-centered Santurce is a land of humble origins. Afro Puerto Ricans, a community whose story is rarely told, were essential to Santurce's establishment. This is one of the reasons I wanted to translate the original title of *San Mateo de Cangrejos, comunidad cimarrona en Puerto Rico* to read as *San Mateo de Cangrejos: Historical* xii | Translator's Note

Notes on a Self-Emancipated Black Community in Puerto Rico. The English translation of the word "cimarron" is "maroon," a word that carries with it the sense of isolation—of a group of people who have escaped enslavement and were then forced to create a separate world that was always in danger of being destroyed. The Black inhabitants of Santurce were both self-emancipated and then officially recognized and allowed to remain free by local authorities. This was a community that was not in hiding and that made efforts to make its presence known as it built a small city with its own monuments and distinct cultural movements. Hence, throughout the volume I have chosen to translate "cimarron" as "self-emancipated."

Understanding San Mateo de Cangrejos/Santurce as a basis for Black culture on the island in the past grounds Afro Puerto Ricans as essential participants in the construction of Puerto Rico. San Mateo de Cangrejos continued to be a central site of Black culture for many decades. It was the birthplace of famed salsa singer Ismael Rivera, a.k.a. "Maelo," the actress/activist Sylvia del Villard, and the great activist/scholar Arturo Alfonso Schomburg. And it was where baseball legends Roberto Clemente and Willie Mays played for the Santurce Cangrejeros.

Since Gilberto Aponte Torres's book points to this Black history in Puerto Rico, it is important to have this scholarship available in more than just its original language. In chapters 1 and 2, this book looks back at who first established San Mateo de Cangrejos and how and why it was established, as well as the central role that it played in centering services for the growing population. Chapter 3 shows how, during the eighteenth and nineteenth centuries, Santurce became a central economic support to the island's most important city—San Juan—and how it increased its own chances of survival. In chapter 4, the fact that Santurce was populated with people of African descent and that this led to it being faced with political and economic difficulties from government authorities that other growing villages and cities often did not have to deal with, is examined. Chapter 5 shows how Santurce's Black population played a major role in protecting Puerto Rico from foreign invasions: because any invasion via the bay of Cangrejos could lead straight to the capital city, local Black populations were required to aid in the military defense of San Juan. Chapter 6 covers the suppression of Cangrejos in 1862, which developed as a result of many reasons—among them urban expansion from San Juan and the transformation of Cangrejos's economy. Chapter 7 looks at how Cangrejos's residents, a noteworthy criminal element, and local authorities functioned in the nineteenth century. Chapter 8 examines the racial and social characteristics assigned to Cangrejos's residents by authorities in San Juan. And chapter 9 looks back at the trajectory of Santurce's urban and demographic development. The photos used in this translation of Gilberto Aponte Torres's book did not appear in the original work. I looked for visual images that could help readers envision the environment Afro Puerto Ricans found themselves in as they established Cangrejos. The updated bibliography at the end of the book is designed to be a helpful source for recommended further readings.

Foreword to the Translation

VANESSA K. VALDÉS

My introduction to San Mateo de Cangrejos was by way of initial research into Arturo Alfonso Schomburg. In her 1989 biography of him, Elinor Des Verney Sinnette writes, "Records in Puerto Rico indicate that Schomburg was baptized in the capital city, San Juan, having been born on January 24, 1874, and was raised in Cangrejos, a section of the city now known as Santurce" (7).[2] In *Diasporic Blackness: The Life and Times of Arturo Alfonso Schomburg* (2017), I wrote that he was born in the capital, unwittingly ignoring a rich history of what Sinnette had categorized as a section of that city.[3] I had been so focused on his life in the United States, I had not done my due diligence in examining his roots in Puerto Rico. Evelyne Laurent-Perrault set me right; she categorizes Mr. Schomburg the "quintessential maroon" in a 2020 essay of that name, and in doing so, she underscores the legacies of the land in which he was born.[4]

It is not enough to say that Mr. Schomburg was Puerto Rican but more specifically, a *cangrejero*, born in the only town that had been founded by *cimarrones* fleeing from the surrounding islands of the then-Danish West Indies primarily, escaping to the freedom guaranteed by the Spanish crown in the seventeenth century. Two hundred years later, Mary Joseph made the same journey. A free Black woman, she lived in Puerto Rico as a laborer, and gave birth to her son Arturo Alfonso in its capital. In translating this volume for us, Karen Juanita Carrillo makes available for an English-reading audience the history of a geographical site dedicated

xvi | Foreword to the Translation

to Black liberation. It is an act of recovery. We glimpse the lives of Black human beings who endeavored to create and maintain a space released from hemispheric denials of their humanity. We are inspired to learn more, to continue, as Mr. Schomburg said, digging up our past.[5]

Prologue to the Original

Santurce Cangrejos. Placing these two names together brings back memories of the history of baseball and of the history of our capital. An entire generation lived through the heated rivalry between the Cangrejeros and their opponents, the San Juan Senators. Santurce Cangrejos: the radio would be turned on and set up in the corner of the cafeteria for the final series, passionate commentaries would be made, and religious promises to keep if your team won—this is a picture of what the most populated section of the capital looked like in the 1950s.

Because there was a team known as the "Cangrejeros," the people of Santurce understand that back then there was a separate city, with a distinct name. There was a church that we could point to as a symbol of that time, San Mateo. There were names—Machuchal, Seboruco—that the elders mentioned from time to time, and not without nostalgia because at that time the children of the recently established professionals in McLeary or in Loíza came to these areas, curious to see bomba dances.

As Santurce grew, memories of Cangrejos began disappearing as well as the sand dunes, the fishing nets, the Santomeñas wearing their gowns at the early St. George mass, the Loíza carts pulled by baying horses with old drivers shouting "Move! Move!" throughout the streets. In the cemetery of Villa Palmera, they were burying those who remembered old Cangrejos—those who recalled when it didn't have paved roads or cars; the Baldorioty express arrived and so did the tourists. They cut the trees on Park Avenue, Santurce became a problem because it was not created under any kind of urban planning. While San Juan had received the careful attention of the Institute of Culture, Santurce became a jungle of unshaded parking lots, abandoned lots, latticed houses, and shuttered businesses.

xviii | Prologue to the Original

Today we see glimpses of a renaissance in Santurce. And one good sign of this reawakening is this historical essay about the old town of Cangrejos by Gilberto Aponte Torres. This fellow historian wanted to look back at the historical experiences of his neighbors, and in this, his first book, he shows us the fruits of his research in archives and libraries. His research is reinforced by his enthusiastic belief that the history of Puerto Rico must come from the people. In this book we find our ancestors overflowing with hidden gems about musicians and filling the annals of our sports. Understanding that the Cangrejeros have their own history is the central reason this researcher is pushing for the revitalization of Santurce.

In this Peoples' History series, we are able to uncover the history of this village that—even though it lost its official status as a town in 1862—has not lost its identity.

Fernando Picó
December 1984

Acknowledgments

Author's Acknowledgments

I would like to acknowledge Luís de la Rosa, Arnoldo Licier, Carlos Rodríguez, Gregorio Villegas, Fernando Picó, Esteban Ramos, Jaime Pérez, Juan Álvarez, Pedro Giusti, Zoraida Fiestta, Padre Párroco, Nicanor Valdez, Salesiano Candido Geada, and Norma Maurosa.

Translator's Acknowledgments

I would like to acknowledge the love and support of my family: Dr. Lisa J. Scott, Sanaa, and Mateo. And I want to sincerely thank my father, Manuel Carrillo Sr.; mother, Dr. Juanita Carrillo; and brother, Manuel Carrillo Jr. for always insisting that I respect and adore our rich Puerto Rican heritage.

Abbreviations

AGPR   Archivo General de Puerto Rico (General Archives of Puerto Rico)

CIH   Centro de Investigaciones Históricas, Universidad de Puerto Rico (Center for Historical Investigations, University of Puerto Rico)

MSJ   Municipio de San Juan (Municipality of San Juan)

HCP   Hemeroteca y Colección Puertorriqueña de la Biblioteca General, Universidad de Puerto Rico (Puerto Rican Collection of the Main Library, University of Puerto Rico)

Introduction

How does one bring a new analysis to the history of a municipality? How do you explain the daily dynamics and escape the constant retelling of the grand political feats of great men, the past mayors and the bishops? How do you enliven that everyday outline usually told to us about such and such a specific year, the locations where things were founded, the names of the founders, the environment of the city, the names of the village, city, or town; place, hermitage, or shore? The concept behind this work is not to challenge that way of retelling history, but to see and analyze the municipality from another, more dynamic and historic perspective. This work is an attempt to study the human foundations that gave impetus to the rise of a municipality, without falling for the traps others have fallen for as they have solely searched for a singular point of foundation or origins. The subject of this study is the people in relation to the city.

The municipal boundary, or district, as it was then called, that we are studying here is that of San Mateo de Cangrejos, whose boundaries actually include Santurce, Isla Verde and Hato Rey. Which social classes lived in Cangrejos? What were the roles played by whites, Blacks, mixed-race people, Africans, and the enslaved in the social structure of Cangrejos? How did all of these different people get along with each other? What did they do for a living, and how did they live in the district? What was the demographic structure of Cangrejos's society?

This work looks at the city's development, as seen as a reflection of the district and of the region. This constitutes an effort to relate the ultimate development of the area with the dynamic that has been attributed to the capitol (San Juan), Cangrejos, and Río Piedras—the centers of

1

today's urban infrastructure. Ultimately, my aim is to show the unity among various areas and to look at how they have interacted. In doing so, I want to show the dynamic of the municipality where the average citizen is the author of, and not the witness to, history. By examining this primary network of social organization—the municipality—we will understand the power of the dominant classes.

The municipality is the basic administrative unit of the colonial administration. As such, the documentation it generates is relevant to our social history: "It is the documentation generated in the administrative cell of what was a small town where we can find true Puerto Rican history. The municipality forges, determines and reflects the character of the people who make and move history." Of course, there are other institutions that also produce documentation, such as the church and central government agencies. But it is in the town where we find the social and economic structures in the flesh and observe the actions of the dominant group on the dominated group. The Cangrejos district is no exception to this rule.

With little wealth or population and no urban development, Cangrejos epitomizes the non-Hispanic Caribbean presence in Puerto Rico. Fugitives from slavery on the islands of St. Eustatius, St. Thomas, and Saint Croix are believed to be among the core population of the original Cangrejeros who were granted lands for cultivation. The laws that recognized the freedom of these self-emancipated people—which date from 1664, 1680, and 1693—effectively legalized this maroon society; they were similar to free Black societies found in Cuba and elsewhere in the Caribbean. Cangrejos epitomizes the potential of an organized Black society in Puerto Rico, with its own social, economic, cultural, familial, and demographic features. To a certain extent, Cangrejos is the border between Puerto Rico and the Caribbean.

Chapter 1

San Mateo de Cangrejos's Origins

San Mateo de Cangrejos is one of the oldest continuously populated areas on the island of Puerto Rico.[1] The site dates back to the seventeenth century, when people first began referring to Cangrejos as a town established by formerly enslaved people who had originally lived in Puerto de Tierra and who were from non-Spanish-speaking territories. Cangrejos has been inhabited for such a long period of time that the conventional notion that Europeans from other nations created and populated all of Puerto Rico's urban centers—needs to be reevaluated.

To understand how Cangrejos developed, we need to look at the data that has emerged from the research about the historical development of San Juan. But to limit this study solely to the area of Cangrejos would make this an incomplete, superficial job. Research shows that the themes that emerge relating to Cangrejos are free Blacks, the central highway, the streetcar, Ubarri, overcrowding in the city, Puerto de Tierra, and military service. And each of these themes links the history of Cangrejos with the development of San Juan.

"The modern city of Puerto Rico had been definitively established by the year 1521, it consisted of about 80 houses, and practically all of them were made of wood."[2] Residents were relocated from Caparra, the island's original capital city settlement, and that led to the urban development of the colony. "The principal feature of the early years of urban development in the city are when it begins to grow monumentally at the start. The profits from mining as the colonization period began led to the proposal for large-scale works."[3] The city would keep growing, as long as the mining

4 | San Mateo de Cangrejos

boom sustained its economic expansion. But during the sixteenth and seventeenth centuries, after this initial expansion, the city suffered a slow and painful growth. Its population was very small, and it did not generate the wealth necessary for the island's development. The city was gradually transformed into a strategic military fortress—designed to serve Spain's Caribbean and American interests. Spain would also turn to Mexico for its military purposes. This was when the walling off of the islet of San Juan Bautista began and when it started to become a military fortress.

"The size of the urban core in the late sixteenth century was drastically reduced. They were surrounded by mountains, groves, palm trees, coconut trees, and lots of fruit trees among which a livestock of free Blacks grazed."[4] The principal urban improvements in the city were military in nature. The result of encircling the city was that the city was not able to withstand any increase in population inside of its walls. Its physical and environmental space and accessibility to housing and land became serious problems for the commercial and administrative center of San Juan. The island-city, because it had little territorial space, had to provide food, meat, coal, fish, rice, and so on to its inhabitants through foreign trade or trade with other towns or villages who sold assorted foods to city residents. This is how Cangrejos came to sell its products to San Juan.

Another major element that led to population growth outside of San Juan's city walls was the small migrant movement that began in the seventeenth century among self-emancipated Africans from neighboring Danish, English, and Dutch territories.[5] Authorities had three options: to re-enslave these people in Puerto Rico, return them to the islands where they had been originally enslaved, or grant them freedom and allow them to stay in Puerto Rico. "A royal *cedula* issued in the year 1664 promised to release all the enslaved Africans of non-Spanish-speaking territories. Enslaved Africans fleeing from other European New World territorial possessions had started arriving on the island in search of freedom around the mid-17th century."[6] It must be noted that the Spanish decree sought several things: to try to encourage population growth on the island, to weaken the position of Spain's enemies in the New World, and to promote the growth of agriculture on the island.

The push to encourage immigration was in large part because there were few people on the island and because "in the years of 1663 and 1680 the King of Spain declared freedom for all self-emancipated Blacks from English and Dutch colonies who sought asylum in Spanish domains," including, of course, Puerto Rico. Prior to this, those countries had signed treaties to return any fugitives from slavery to their countries of origin.

But freedom was not the only thing on offer in Puerto Rico—a place where African slavery was still in practice; men who accepted the offer were ceded "two acres of land for use on the part of the island now known by the name Puerta de Tierra."[7] Even though in Puerta de Tierra, "due to the land's low fertility, authorities agreed that the Black settlers could pass through and across the Puerta de Tierra bridge . . . and populate land as far as up to the Martín Peña canal."[8] This led to a population increase of self-emancipated Africans in areas like Cangrejos with people who devoted themselves to farming and selling their crops in San Juan. Puerta de Tierra, on the other hand, had another serious problem, which was not just the fertility of its soil, but the fact that it had been initially established inside of a military fortress.[9]: It was "subject to strict military rules, with carefully regulated building heights because they were in the field of fire of the battery enclosure in the east of the city."[10]

Figure 1.1. Porto-Rico.

6 | San Mateo de Cangrejos

Figure 1.2. Porto-Rico with Cangrejos focus.

Overcrowding inside the city walls, the arrival of self-emancipated Africans, Puerta de Tierra's barren earth, the fortified military area, the incentives to create the settlement, and the supply needs of the urban market led to population growth outside of the walled city as well as across the San Antonio canal and up to the Martín Peña canal. This is why the San Mateo de Cangrejos district developed during the seventeenth century with free Blacks in Puerto Rico, people who became creolized under the Spanish crown and later under the government of Puerto Rico.

How many refugees, freedmen, or fugitive enslaved Africans came from English, Danish, or Dutch colonies—especially from the English and Danish colonies? We do not know, but there were frequent arrivals. According to José Colombán Rosario y Justina, "by 1714 Puerto Rico already had an aggregate of 80 self-liberated Africans from Saint Croix, who had been granted their freedom by the authorities as long as they agreed to be baptized and to remain loyal to the monarchy."[11] A series of royal decrees spoke of organizing and consolidating a colony of the now free, formerly enslaved people on the island. On October 2, 1738, a report looked into "whether it was profitable to bring Black fugitives from foreign islands to a village, and what it may cost."[12] There was also concern that some people would try to re-enslave the self-liberated Africans. In 1750, the king ordered "that those enslaved Africans who freed themselves from the English and Dutch colonies and took refuge in Spain's domains and have embraced our holy Catholic faith, under no pretext or any cause can be sold as some have tried to do . . . whether in peacetime or in war. . . . they will be free."[13]

On July 7, 1763, it was ordered that based on the referral of the "testimony of the priest of the Saint Croix Catholic Church concerning the restitution of the enslaved who came here to become Christians, and have been so informed."[14] No wonder the free Black population of Cangrejos was increasing. Yet we should not see or interpret Cangrejos as the place where Spain practiced a form of humanitarian politics. Even though by the end of the eighteenth century, treaties had been signed for the return of self-emancipated Blacks to their native island, by May 12, 1801, auctions of enslaved Africans were canceled on the island of Saint Croix, the auctioneers were refunded, and the refugees were allowed to remain.[15]

Iñigo Abad described the Cangrejos of 1770 in these terms: "At a distance of three quarters of a mile from the bridge, along the seacoast to the east, is the town of San Mateo de Cangrejos, whose inhabitants are Black. . . . [T]hey have been given land—even though the land is a bit sandy—so that they can grow their own yuca, beans, rice and other vegetables and trade it in the city."[16] This description inspires a reflection: Cangrejos represented an alternative human settlement to the historiography of the *Cédula de Gracias* that aimed to establish migratory flows. These were not immigrants with capital, but people who were associated with smuggling and privateering and who could present a possible support to those who were resisting slavery on the island. This was Guillermo Baralt's conclusion when he stated that "an insurrection of Blacks could have disastrous results for the inhabitants of this area, and in particular for the capital. On top of which, El Roble was just at the south of the Cangrejos district, a hiding place for self-liberated Africans and other Black people." The Black population's prevalence in Cangrejos is clearly stated in the censuses of the last third of the eighteenth century. Baralt, analyzing one of these censuses, points out that "in Cangrejos, the racial disproportion was even more critical than in Río Piedras. The population was 460 free Blacks, 127 free mulattoes, 99 enslaved Blacks and only 123

8 | San Mateo de Cangrejos

whites. Racial disproportions like this did not go unnoticed by the authorities. From the first moment Blacks were brought to America, the Spanish authorities were always aware of the problem, since this was the primary condition that would facilitate the start of a revolt by enslaved Blacks."[17]

Chapter 2

The Church of Cangrejos

Spanish authorities used various terms to refer to the growing settlements in the area: words like *town, village, riverside,* and *locale.* They also used phrases like *in the margins, near,* and *proximity* to identify a settlement with a river or a coast whose presence furthered the economic activity of the first settlers. Sometimes they used names that recalled the previous presence of indigenous populations: for example, the name *Seboruco,* which is found in the Santurce neighborhood, seems to be a corruption of the indigenous *sibaorucu,* which means rocky hills.

Some of the economic activities that spurred early settlements in Puerto Rico were the sugar mills, yuca crops, gold mining activities in the rivers, and fishing. But there was another active element to promote the creation of urban cores: the chapels, which served the developing populations' religious and spiritual needs, were also a stimulus to further population growth.

Cangrejos, with its cabins and huts made of straw and palm leaves, had a chapel—or church—in its original urban center. We do not know its first site, but it was certainly a central element in the official religious culture of the village's self-emancipated Africans. The chapel promoted the stability of the population and served to help the development of their integration into Creole society.

Jorge David Díaz notes that because of where the chapels were placed, we "know the island's first population centers, and the places that were becoming important in the development of Puerto Rico."[1] So the chapels had two basic functions. They were created to represent the hierarchical Catholic Church in that town and to service the population in its surroundings. Díaz describes the first rural chapels and chaplaincies that served as "the backbone of the church during the first centuries . . . [I]t was through their managers, and chaplains, that the ecclesiastical history of Puerto Rico was developed."[2] The chapel of Cangrejos helped integrate Caribbean Blacks into the new realities of the island: the Catholic religion, the Castilian language, religious festivals, and local customs. Even though the mentality of the church was colonial and conservative, it was an institution that ended up aiding the cultural integration of different sectors of society.

In 1729, Bishop Sebastian Lorenzo Pizarro reported, "I found chapels in Cangrejos (Santurce), Manatí, Rincón, Mayagüez, Cabo Rojo, Yauco, Caguas and Las Piedras."[3] Even though this helps note the growth of the settlement, it was not until 1773 that Cangrejos separated from Río Piedras to become its own district. Governor Miguel de Muesas separated the two based on a recommendation.[4] Eventually, the new municipality grew to have distinct neighborhoods like Cangrejos Arriba (now Isla Verde), Machucahal (Loíza Street), Bridge (Parada 26 and Barrio Obrero), Seboruco (Villa Palmeras), and Hato del Rey. The religious headquarters of the municipality became what is the present-day Church of San Mateo.

Figure 2.1. Church of San Mateo de Cangrejos.

Chapter 3

Economic Activity in Cangrejos in the Eighteenth and Nineteenth Centuries

The economy in Cangrejos started out with basic foodstuffs, like the planting of yuca and other staple crops, alongside fishing. It was a subsistence economy, but it generated enough of a surplus to justify a regular presence in the San Juan market. Other sources of income seem to have been raising cattle and selling coal and firewood.[1] Here is the testimony of Andre-Pierre Ledru, in 1797: "The inhabitants of Cangrejos, almost all of whom are Black or 'mulatto,' have purchased their freedom with their industry and they are enjoying it. Although they have only arid soil, they have been able to grow many fruits and vegetables for the consumers in San Juan. This small village has only some 1800 houses and 700 inhabitants."[2]

Cangrejos was practically surrounded by water everywhere: the bay, the San Antonio canal, Lake County, the Martín Peña canal, Lake Cangrejos (San José), and the Atlantic Ocean. It was only natural, therefore, that a fishing industry developed and that in some places the authorities auctioned off fishing rights. The proceedings of the town council of San Juan documented the existence in Cangrejos of fishing yards.

In 1735, Ignacio Muriel made a request to the San Juan town council "asking to rent the base of the Martín Peña canal, which goes as far as the sea, for fifty *reales* by ordinance the amount that is assigned to this city."[3] Such leases were often a source of conflict. As in 1777, "Bernardo Calderon presented himself [to the Council] to stop Francisco Chiclana from using an area which goes all the way to the lake, near his plot, from

12 | San Mateo de Cangrejos

the Martín Peña canal, and he requested that the cattleman Don Pizzaro recognize his property."[4] The council decided that he could not have the property, "except during specific times, and this would only be allowed to Mr. Calderon, the tenant, within the league, based on his urgent need to care for meats as has been frequently experienced in recent months."[5]

Another case involving city supplies is the request of Andrés de Santana to city hall to allow him "the sale of fish as a lessee of the Laguna yard, a *real* and a half, and with respect to the represent causal, was bestowed with the precise fact which is to bring this city to its sale."[6] On another occasion,

> Juan Meléndez, José Caba and Jacinto and Francisco Catalán were presented before a government tribunal where a memorial was held, which this Honorable Member of the Council wishes to report. During this memorial it was made known that the Martín Peña occupant . . . prevents them from fishing in this Lagoon. To which the Council reported the following: That the lessee of the Martín Peña canal can only allow those who have been permitted in the lagoon and that no one else can fish within this area unless given permission. These lagoons, bays, and river mouths are for private fishing with nets or hammocks because these are fish-breeding routes and overfishing would annihilate them.[7]

There were also interventions made by the Dominican religious order in regards to fishing: "Another letter was presented by the Prior and (convent) of Santo Domingo opposing the lands granted to Domingo Canales, for the damage that it would have on Cangrejos Arriba, and which suggested that two acres of land should be provided for sheltering the corral and to suspend the grant of land made to Domingo Canales and his pretense to justify his self-importance."[8]

But it is alleged that in 1782 "the religious order of Santo Domingo had no right to make comments about the pond or corral in Boca de Cangrejos, or it would affect their role as Public Exchequer."[9]

The importance of fishing, as well as of fishing routes, as a source of income is illustrated by the following:

Table 3.1a. Leases of passages and river estuaries, 1761, 1765, and 1819

| | Fish amounts at auction | | |
Name of the Yard or Passage	1761	1765	1819
Palo Seco	838	400	3,000
Loysa	128	210	460
Martin Pena	32	100	150
Boca Havana	80	61	708 y 1/3
Boca de Toa	5	102	
Pueblo Viejo	12½	10	575 1/3
Boca Jacagua		25	
Boca Arecibo		13	
Boca Manati		10	
Boca de Sibuco		21	41 2/3
Toa Baxa			12
Rio de la Sabana			1
Guayanes			262/3
Faxardo			22/3
Corral de Cerdos			61 2/3

Source: Proceedings of the San Juan Town Council and Record, 1819 in AGPR. Spanish Government Fund, box 559.

In table 3.1a, you can see the value given to the plots and passageways over the course of time. This gives an idea of the importance that fisheries had in Cangrejos during this period.

Another important section of the relations of the San Juan Town Council with the residents of the villages is the supply of capital market meat. The cattle quotas assigned to the various districts were the subject of long discussions, some of which show that the district of Cangrejos provided supplies in emergencies.[10]

The effort of supplying other products to the capital is also reflected in town council minutes of 1773, which point to the importance of the yuca of Cangrejos and Loíza to the daily diet:

> Somewhere there could be a place to supply and subsidize these
> public needs and livelihoods based on the peace of the country,

commonly known as yuca bread, because the small amount of the crop that is on the island of this fruit, limited to parties in Loysa and Cangrejos, is insufficient for the consumption of more than one hundred and twenty thousand people who compose it, and often hurricanes have destroyed and ruined these plantings, leaving everyone . . . therefore subject to the effects of extreme need.[11]

For Cangrejos to be able to overcome a primitive and marginal economy, there had to be more developments. In the 18th century the population was not large and economic activity was slow. The area needed a better communication system, and there needed to be a clearing and distribution of herds and wastelands to help stimulate agricultural production. In the words of the San Juan council, "the best and only way to achieve this quickly is to demolish the breeding herds, buildings in the vicinity and the fertile lands and to at least create ranches to plant cotton, coffee, achiote, snuff, ginger, cocoa, anil and other fruits useful to the Real Compañía and as groceries for the supply of this area."[12] So in 1757, the council ordered that "in the first term of two months, come September and October, all breeding herds within the immediate parts of this city will be demolished, namely, Toa Alta and Baxa, Bayamón, Guaynabo, Río Piedras and Cangrejos."[13]

In the 1765 census, Cangrejos and Río Piedras appeared to have a wealth of livestock: 63 horses, 33 pigs, 27 goats, one mule, 132 oxen, cows and steers, and two donkeys.[14] In 1775, Cangrejos reported a herd, 46 ranches, 832 cotton bushes, 1160 coffee trees, 9 cane stalks, 211 heads of cattle, 7 mules, 126 horses, and cattle less. The annual production is estimated at 30 pounds of cotton, 40 pounds of coffee, 24 pounds of rice, 49 cattle, 3 horses, and 18 colts.[15]

In the nineteenth century, the economy starts to look better. In 1812, Cangrejos reported 26½ cords of grass, 54 cane stalks, three stalks of bananas, 298 oxen, 172 horses, and 167 calves. The production included seven quintals of coffee, 44 bushels of rice, six bushels of corn, and a GDP of 2.218 pesos in jars of molasses, 17 oxen in pesos, 43 pesos in horses, 5 pesos in mules and 182 pesos in calves.[16]

Economic Activity in Cangrejos | 15

In 1818, there are 80 storeowners with 34 stalls (6,800 strings in accord with the arithmetic measured at 83 cords per owner), there are 137 houses, two wood mills, three iron mills, the latter valued at 3,000 pesos each. Plantings consist of 79 sugar cane stalks, one coffee bush, 11 straws of rice, 2½ banana stalks, 2½ corn stalks, 18½ stalks of yucca. There are 140 cows, 98 oxen, three steers for fattening, 70 mares, 13 foals, 96 horses, 14 mules, 13 pigs, 40 sheep, and three donkeys.[17] The estimated amount of production was 1575 quintals of sugar, 12 pounds of coffee, 88 bushels of rice, 187½ loads of bananas, 10 corn bundles, 2300 jars of molasses, and 80 quarts of rum barrels. Yuca is valued at an estimated 925 pesos, and there are also a reported eight bundles of vegetables. The young animals numbered 42 calves, 13 horses, two mules, 38 pigs, 10 sheep, and a donkey.[18]

The amount of municipal property wealth in 1818 is summarized in table 3.1b.

Out of all the production, sugar and molasses are the most profitable; their combined value exceeds by four to one the price of other lines of production (see table 3.2).

Undoubtedly, though production was diversified, the majority of what was produced was dominated by derivatives of sugar cane. But cane sowing was not the most common activity for residents. So in 1826, Mayor Eusebio Noa disclosed to the governor of the tower that in relation to the economy of Cangrejos, "these people are as miserable as they are plaintive," that "I have visited the houses of the neighbors to find out what they are doing and which crops they are planting, but all of them claim to be charcoal vendors."[19]

Table 3.1b. Total value table

	Pesos	**% Of total value**
Total value of the mills	10.400	17.3
Total value of homes	15.618	26
Total value of land	<u>34.000</u>	56.6
	60.018	

16 | San Mateo de Cangrejos

Table 3.2. Value and relative importance of agrofishing production in Cangrejos, 1818

Products	Pesos	% of total value
Sugar	8,250	56.5
Coffee	190	1.3
Rice	308	2.1
Plantains	187 1/2	1.2
Corn	30	.2
Yuca	925	6.3
Melao	3,450	23.6
Rum	855	5.8
Livestock	393	2.6
	14,588.5	

Source: AGPR, Archivo General de Puerto Rico (General Archives of Puerto Rico), box 429.

Cangrejos's Wealth in the Nineteenth Century, by Neighborhood

Wealth censuses regarding the district of San Mateo de Cangrejos show us a diversified economy in terms of agricultural and livestock activity, even though Cangrejos was in large part a subsistence economy. Lists of grants and public expenditures help us understand the particular dynamic of the five boroughs San Mateo was separated into: Cangrejos Arriba, Machuchal, Puente, Seboruco, and Hato del Rey. With this quantitative data, we can analyze the wealth of each district by outlining the funds people had to pay and the degree of settlements according to the number of heads of households. Unfortunately, there is no complete series available, but we can summarize the data based on the years we do have available (see table 3.3).

In this table several characteristics stand out. The number of families in Cangrejos Arriba was in decline between 1820 and 1837. Machuchal and Seboruco also show a decline up until 1825; that decline strengthened in 1827, and in 1830 it showed another increase. The Puente neighborhood shows a surprising increase for 1827, which soon came to an end.

Table 3.4 summarizes the municipal revenue by quarter, according to records of public expenditure. The figures represent the total weights and actual contributions paid by the neighborhoods.

Economic Activity in Cangrejos | 17

Table 3.3. Number of heads of households in Cangrejos, 1820–1866

Neighborhood	1820	1824	1825	1827	1830	1837	1866
Cangrejos Arriba	42	31	30	28	24	19	33
Machuchal	47	34	33	36	34	57	—
Del Puente	33	28	30	68	33	39	58
Seboruco34	27	28	—	—	—	—	
Hato del Rey	30	34	28	32	31	31	22

Source: AGPR, Archivo General de Puerto Rico (General Archives of Puerto Rico), box 429.

Table 3.4. Municipal income for public expenditures in Cangrejos, 1820–1832

Neighborhood	1820	1824	1825	1827	1830	1832
Cangrejos Arriba	49.6	59.2	64.6	87.7	59.4	42⅓
Machuchal	95.0	39.3	44.0	46.2	81.6	77.4
Del Puente	127	38.1	40.2	96.0	42.3	45.7
Seboruco	177	31.4	41.0			
Hato del Rey	293.6	349.3	360.3	317.2	280.7	285½

Source: AGPR, Archivo General de Puerto Rico (General Archives of Puerto Rico), box 429, public expenditure records.

The richest neighborhood of all the districts is undoubtedly Hato del Rey. Its wealth was not due to the number of taxpaying families who established themselves there because, as can be seen in table 3.3, that number was not greater than that of other neighborhoods. It probably had to do with the importance of its agricultural activities, particularly its sugarcane crops. A summary of the total quarters allowance (tax contributed to the treasury of Puerto Rico) stresses the economic dominance of Hato del Rey (see table 3.5).

In 1842, Cangrejos had a population of 1,035 residents, of which there were 850 laborers, three carpenters, one mason, three blacksmiths, three coopers, three merchants, and seven small markets. There are 1000 forestland acres, 6600 acres of grassland, 25 houses and 172 shacks, two wood mills and two iron mills, and two stills. The total value of the property is estimated at 39,755 pesos.[23]

18 | San Mateo de Cangrejos

Table 3.5. Subsidy payments in Cangrejos, by neighborhood, 1825–1832

Neighborhood	1825	1827	1830	1832
Cangrejos Arriba	80.2	10.3	72.4	51.6
Machuchal	55	192	99.2	95.4
Seboruco	51.2	256	—	—
Del Puente	52	266.2	320	56.4
Hato del Rey	453.4	641.2	342.4	351.6

Note: This does not include contributions from stores and galleries. *Source:* AGPR, Archivo General de Puerto Rico (General Archives of Puerto Rico), box 429, public expenditure records.

Plantings reported are summarized in table 3.6.

Land planted with sugarcane tended to dominate the valuation of farming land. But sugarcane was not the only source of income. That same report mentions 1,090 coconut palms, valued at 3200 pesos. In addition, there is a lime kiln priced at 80 pesos, 10 orange trees (5 pesos), and 30 avocado trees (4 pesos).

In general, the data from 1842 shows an underdeveloped Cangrejos, in contrast to the increased agriculture and commerce that had already taken place in other municipalities. The circulation of money appears to have been limited. Cangrejos had stopped growing coffee, and there are no reports that tobacco, yam, beans, cotton, or vegetables were being planted. Perhaps area residents did not have access to the credit that was available in other areas. If not, why was there such a decline in Cangrejos's economy?

Table 3.6. Cultivated lands and their estimated value in Cangrejos, 1842

Cultivations	Length in acres	Value in pesos
Sugarcane	50	2,200
Plantains	2	20
Rice	2	6
Corn	4	12
Yuca	10	38
Potatoes	6	60

Source: AGPR, Archivo General de Puerto Rico (General Archives of Puerto Rico), military subjects, box 261, records of Cangrejos.

Economic Activity in Cangrejos | 19

There was a decrease in livestock breeding and in the value of cattle. Poultry appears to have been a main source of subsistence. Table 3.7 summarizes the animals reported in 1842.

These animals produced offspring valued at 880 pesos, or some 14.1% of their value. In comparison are the 2,336 pesos quoted as the price for cultivated land rented for 1,937 pesos, which is 82.9% of its value.[20] (These figures do not include the 500,000 coconuts valued at 300 pesos because that report included the value of the palms planted.) This contrast seems to show that agriculture was generally more profitable than raising animals, but you have to remember that out of 1,835 pesos of agricultural rent, some 94.7% came from the 50 planted sugar cane stalks. As in the previous generation, only a minority of the farmers derived an income from cane sugar, and most lived off of their crops, from their animal breeding and fishing activities and from the preparation of coal.

The nearest economic data available for Cangrejos is for the year 1862; at this time, the activities that generate wealth in the district have changed. The area has begun to urbanize because of its proximity to the capital, the opening of the main highway in 1852, and the establishment of aquatic lines of communication. To determine the wealth in the district of Cangrejos in 1862, we calculate in table 3.8.

In 1862, the Hato del Rey neighborhood was still the wealthiest,

Table 3.7. Animals reported in Cangrejos in 1842

Animals	Value in pesos
200 cows	3,000
80 oxen	1,600
80 horses	1,280
10 mares	160
1 donkey	20
2 mules	50
10 pigs	40
200 chickens	75
4 turkeys	4
Total	6,2229

Source: AGPR, Archivo General de Puerto Rico (General Archives of Puerto Rico), military affairs, box 261, records of Cangrejos.

20 | San Mateo de Cangrejos

Table 3.8. Wealth in Cangrejos in 1862

Neighborhood of Cangrejos	Municipality from which it was annexed	Value in pesos	Number of residents
Pueblo and Puente	San Juan	20,605	58
Cangrejos Arriba	Carolina	6,450	33
Hato del Rey	Rio Piedras	30,235	22
Totals		57,290	113

Source: AGPR, Archivo General de Puerto Rico (General Archives of Puerto Rico), Development, file 57, box 147, record 22, 1866.

even though it had the least amount of people. Cangrejos Arriba, which today is Isla Verde, was the poorest area. The gradual displacement of livestock and agriculture as sources of wealth is reflected in data for 1862 (see table 3.9).

The economic transformation of Cangrejos, then in progress, was a reflection of the activity of certain dominant individuals. In 1864, ownership of land in Cangrejos that was annexed by San Juan testifies to the presence of landowners who had connections—in contrast with the vast majority of Cangrejos' residents (see table 3.10).

Table 3.9. Sources of wealth in Cangrejos, 1862

Number of contributors	Source of wealth	Tax share (pesos)	Capital reported	Proceeds received (pesos)	% of the total product	% of output to capital
11	Industrial	73.70	8,600	1,474	29	17.1
16	Commercial	38	1,375	1,160	22.8	73.6
—	Fishing	6	330	120	2.3	36.3
19	Agriculture	12.73	2,700	835	16.8	31.6
10	Urban	73.38	17,360	1,466	28.8	8.4
Totals						
36		233.73	30,365	3,075		

Note: The industrial wealth included a dairy, a liquor store, a pottery workshop, and a cabinetmaker's workshop. The commercial wealth came from grocery stores and small markets. *Source:* AGPR, Archivo General de Puerto Rico (General Archives of Puerto Rico), Development Series, folder 57, box 147, file 22, year 1866.

Table 3.10. Land tenure in the parts of Cangrejos annexed to San Juan, 1864

Number of Owners	Size of the properties	Total width of lands
6	100 to 315 acres	995 acres
67	1 to 65 acres	794 acres

Source: AGPR, Archivo General de Puerto Rico (General Archives of Puerto Rico), Development Series, folder 57, file 22, 1864, San Mateo de Cangrejos.

The contrast between six owners who own 55.6% of the land in Cangrejos annexed to the capital and the 67 who share the rest shows the dynamics of urban development in the area in the following decades.

Chapter 4

Ethnic Origins of
San Mateo de Cangrejos

Ever since the first census was taken on the island chronicling the population and its wealth, there have been distinctions and classifications of the different human elements that make up the demographic structure of the island. The censuses demonstrated the social divisions of the island population. Thus, the census of 1775 is entitled: "State of the Island of Puerto Rico, including the number of their populations; leagues distant from each other: neighbors who have each, with distinction of white, brown, aggregates, free Blacks and slaves. Ranches, Herds, crops and livestock that exist."

Skin color and legal condition were the criteria that distinguished the distinct elements of a society in which there were grand contrasts. Even though daily life was another story, the structures of our national society consecrated distinctions, distance, and legal and judicial separation. Racial distinctions were altering the details about the components of Puerto Rican society: Blacks and whites.

In the case of Cangrejos, we have a town created by free Blacks. This fact breaks with the typical idea of European establishment of towns on the island. Slavery did not take a firm root in Cangrejos, and neither did the white population: free Indigenous people and foreign-born Blacks populated the town. I will analyze, briefly, some of the racial concepts that the census employed to demarcate the racial categories found in San Mateo de Cangrejos.

The classifications most commonly used were those of *moreno, mulato, grifo, zambo,* and *mestizo.* These denominations appeared frequently in sources related to the history of Cangrejos, many of which recognized the predominantly African origin of Cangrejos's population. The chronicler Fernando Miyares González, for example, notes that it was the district of San Mateo de Cangrejos whose "principal neighborhood is of Blacks who farm a sandy earth that produces various roots for maintenance."[1] Cangrejos's troops of free *morenos,* as we will see, were part of the defense of the area of the capital.

Even though fugitive enslaved people were the principal sources of Cangrejos's original population, this source was being wiped out in the eighteenth century because Spain was abiding to its agreements with other European colonial powers and returning fugitive enslaved people. In 1767 "there was a covenant between the government of Spain and Denmark for the mutual restitution of fugitive slaves."[2] In 1791, Spain signed another treaty with Holland to not take in fugitive enslaved people. The first article of this treaty "establishes the reciprocal restitution of white or Black fugitives owned by Spaniards in America and Holland's colonies, particularly among those where complaints of desertion have been more frequent, namely, between Puerto Rico and Sint Eustatius, Coro and Curaçao, the Spanish establishments in the Orinoco, and Esequibo, Demaray, Berbices and Surinam."[3]

Nevertheless, another source of Cangrejos's population were the free Blacks from the area of San Juan, who found the San Mateo district a strategic area that helped them establish themselves. In the parochial books of Cangrejos and Río Piedras, there are frequent mentions of freemen and free Black creoles.

Chapter 5

San Mateo de Cangrejos
and Military Defense

San Mateo de Cangrejos is a unique town in Puerto Rican history because of the nature of its origin, its ethnic composition, and—a fact that every Black Puerto Rican should know—the contributions Blacks from Cangrejos made to the military.

Even though the district of Cangrejos did not have the structures and fortresses that San Juan had, its territory had strategic value. The small bay of Cangrejos was the vulnerable point in the defense system of the capital. From there, various bodies of water led to the bay of San Juan: the lagoon of Vacia Talega, the Suárez stream, the San José lagoon, or the Corozas and the Martín Peña stream. This is how Íñigo Abbad saw it when he wrote that "with little effort the enemy could pass the lagoon where the Martín Peña stream ended, and let himself out in the bay making a joke of the city's fortifications."[1]

One of the conditions self-emancipated Blacks had to comply with while living in Cangrejos was that, when called upon, they had to help provide for the military defense of San Juan. By 1759, Cangrejos had already registered two troops with 120 soldiers, while there were a total of 66 troops and 5,611 soldiers on the entire island.[2] It was Pedro Cortijo, "Captain of the Moreno troop, in the name of 55 *morenos*," who succeeded in separating Cangrejos and Río Piedras in 1773.[3] By the middle of the 1770s, according to Abad, Blacks in Cangrejos and others in the area had become "a group of hunters who are part of this Island's disciplined militia."[4]

In 1797, the British put the capital's system of defense to the test. They disembarked in the Cangrejos bay and utilized the streams to arrive at the trenches, which in Seboruco the military engineer Captain Ignacio Mascaró, had ordered to be built to stop passage from the lagoon to the Martín Peña stream.[5] There, the 3,000 soldiers who disembarked under Abercromby[6] surprised the 92 soldiers of Cangrejos.[7] Mascaró "left the bridge and the Martín Peña stream, abandoning the Seboruco de Barriga. General Abercromby seized all of Cangrejos and cut land communication from the city with the interior of the island."[8] The British used the country house built by Bishop Francisco de la Cuerda in 1793 as Abercromby's headquarters: "This building, situated over the distant hill two leagues from the Capital, and just one league from the sea, seemed to General Abercromby the most suitable because from there he could view the vast horizon, because it dominated the vista and showed the fleet, and from there he could see the movements of the Spaniards."[9] Under these circumstances, "the British who ruled Cangrejos and were very well entrenched in the Martín Peña bridge"[10] sowed the fear that San Juan could fall and be invaded, according to the later testimony of Bishop Zengotita in the districts of Río Piedras, Guaynabo, and Bayamón.[11]

The intervention of urban militias from various parts of the island and the urgent need for supplies changed the situation and forced the British to withdraw from Puerto Rico. But the impact of their attack on Cangrejos was felt immediately and for a long time thereafter. Bishop Zengotita initiated his pastoral visit to Cangrejos in 1797, "where the enemies' army was encamped," and found that the neighbors were "scattered, like fugitives, and all afflicted with the damages and losses that the enemy made. I tried to console them, and even help them regain their faculties. urging them all to return to their farms and homes by all means dictated by prudence."[12]

One hundred and one years later, in 1898, when there was another attack on the island, the Spanish authorities fortified these places: "Once the operations began, a semi-permanent battery was built in Santurce, on top of Seboruco, which, with its splendid range, swept the Martín Peña canal, Río Piedras, Prim hill, the point where the enemy could place their canons: the openings to Cangrejos, where the British landed in the year 1797, and the little island of Miraflores."[13] But, this time, the invasion did not come by way of Cangrejos.

Chapter 6

The Suppression of Cangrejos in 1862

Why was San Mateo de Cangrejos suppressed, and why did it have its territory split up between San Juan, Carolina, and Río Piedras? How did the first town founded by free Blacks and self-emancipated Africans in our national history disappear?

We can consider at least two historical thoughts about the destruction of Cangrejos: the territorial needs of San Juan and the weak economy of Cangrejos. In 1875, the municipal council notes: "Of the great mass of people who live in this Capital and which one notices after much time, mostly in the poorer classes, that they live so oppressed in the lower lying areas which have unhealthy, and little ventilated interiors which could cause epidemic problems for this developing population."[1]

The notes pointed out: "The capital of Puerto Rico, as Your Excellency had occasion to observe it, was encircled in a narrow circle of walls, which completely impeded its development as it was imperiously demanded, the progressive increase of the population, while new constructions of particular buildings lacked space inside."[2]

The people found relief in the neighborhoods outside the city walls. There were auctions, sales, and leases of land for construction of small buildings in the neighborhoods in the military area. The San Juan municipal council requested permission to allow the construction of masonry houses of one level in the districts of Puerto de Tierra, Marina and Carbonera.[3] Obviously, Cangrejos was the next logical point for urban expansion.

28 | San Mateo de Cangrejos

The long-term transformation of Cangrejos's economy was another factor. The investments of those who recently arrived in the area did not necessarily strengthen the already established agrarian infrastructure. The royal treasury still controlled and at times rented out large portions of the land in Cangrejos. Several documented cases show this fact. In 1864, José Aruz requested "permission to transfer a property that he has in the neighborhood of Cangrejos Arriba, owned by the Royal Treasury, to Don José Lopez Noriega . . . for the lease of 250 acres of land."[4] In 1876, there is the mention of some lands "in which the estate is called 'Hato of Cangrejos Arriba' owned by State regulators . . . whose farm has an area of 1,379 leagues according to map created in . . . 1859."[5]

Access to land was not the same for everyone. One notable case was in the partition of Hato del Rey, which Victoriano Rodríguez, a native of the island, requested in 1829 that the mayor give him 33 acres. "The land known as Hato consisted of six mounts and a half of land, 1,300 cords of which were seven parts, and it yielded to as many individuals who had a portion of it." This was an example of the poor distribution of land in different sectors.

In 1862, in the part annexed by San Juan, 73 owners paid taxes on 1,989 acres. In the district of Hato Rey, which was annexed by Río Piedras, 17 taxpayers owned 3,054 acres. These imbalances would go on to influence how the area established its future urban development planning.

On the other hand, the fact that some of its largest landowners were absentee owners created problems for the municipality's stability and reinforced the strength of those who wanted the dissolution and annexation of Cangrejos: "The constant problem of the administration of this so-called town is that it is too weak to take care of its governmental duties . . . because of the lack of elements that are necessary to complete diverse services and public charges."[6]

One of the problems that Cangrejos seemed to have was fiscal. But sources also suggested that racial prejudices played a part. One of these alluded to "the frequency that problems occurred in the construction of the municipal board of Cangrejos . . . [because] this was a community which was almost completely made up of people of color, they could not be relied upon to perform their municipal duties."[7] It also states that "scarce resources have meant that few people populated the area, despite

The Suppression of Cangrejos in 1862 | 29

its being one of the oldest on the island, nor have there been, until now, many of the buildings or public establishments that would be needed to service such a population."[8] Therefore, the opinion was reached that

> a population so scarcely existing and in the vicinity of this City, offers locals and strangers an unfavorable idea about the progress and advancement of the country . . . whose Capital for its growing population which every day takes on more services and facilities to meet the needs of an educated and demanding society, and this may not be corrected without enlarging its boundaries beyond the narrow space of its tactical area, because of this the City cannot really be used, therefore there are no grounds that serve to relieve our large populations and that are intended to form hills and groves for common use.[9]

So, in summary, the commission constituted for this matter by the San Juan municipal council states that "due to the above reasons, and taking also into account the taxes that have to be paid by the citizens of Cangrejos for the expenses and needs required to service the people, and because it has very few citizens to help cover the budget,"[10] Cangrejos should be annexed.

The Royal Order of November 11, 1862, approved the takeover of the town of Cangrejos.[11] In jurisdictional terms, the Martín Peña canal remained with the capital and Río Piedras, San José Lake, and the poor of Canoas with the capital and Carolina. With the takeover of Cangrejos, they had to create, in the area annexed by San Juan, a district mayor for Cangrejos—a role that was occupied from 1864 to 1876 by Pablo Ubarri. Ubarri began to serve as the spokesperson for Cangrejos in San Juan.[12]

Pablo Ubarri was one of the most important people in the social, economic, and political life of Puerto Rico. We see him as an owner of enslaved Black people, land, buildings, and the railroad and president of the Conservative Party. The base for his political influence was Cangrejos, where his properties were located. But various conflicts with members of San Juan's town hall led to the dissolution of the role of district mayor because they determined that it there were two different authorities for the area: Ubarri and the municipal inspector.[13] In legal and jurisdictional

Figure 6.1. Train bridge over the Martin Peña channel, San Juan, Puerto Rico.

terms, there was no reason for the duality since the inspector was the representative at the municipal council, and the district mayor was a temporary position that was being extended indefinitely. In such terms, one councilor argued on the debate: "Cangrejos is not currently recognized as a population that is part of the municipality, which is why the law states that it is ruled by a district mayor."[14] Indeed, there was the idea "that Cangrejos is one of seven districts into which the City is divided, and it was agreed that this was the way to have law and order—to assign to that part of the population an inspector, as one of the many districts."[15]

Faced with conflicting authorities, the neighbors sent letters of support for Pablo Ubarri and the role of district mayor to the municipal council, and these letters were also sent on to the governor. This clearly and without doubt favored the council: "Whereas some twelve years ago Don Pablo Ubarri was appointed delegate to Cangrejos because his services were needed, today the reasons for such needs have ceased therefore this neighborhood has a commissioner and municipal police . . . [T]he Corporation employees maintain public order without the need for a supplement of others."[16] This is why the role of district mayor was done away with in 1876. San Juan, with its demographic and urban growth at the end of the nineteenth century, occupied and developed the annexed lands in 1862.

Chapter 7

The Institutional Order of Cangrejos

There is a national inclination in Puerto Rico to believe that everything in the past was better than what we have in the present. Institutions such as slavery, Prim's Black Code, and Pezuela's "Day Laborers' Book" (La Libreta del Jornalero), among others, would make any view of the past look pretty violent and brutal. The idyll of the past does little damage to our historical documents, but has damaged the minds of some of Puerto Rico's historians: there is no idyllic past, but there is a past that was not investigated that is full of sources that have not been consulted. Cangrejos has certain characteristics that indicate a violent and unstable territory where institutional harmony, in light of the data, is little more than a fallacy.

Cangrejos's municipal government was unstable, which helps us understand the lack of attention the inhabitants paid to authorities during that time. In turn, this instability could explain the emergence of criminal acts in the agricultural sector, where the number of farmers far exceeded that of enslaved people and laborers. The neighborhoods were isolated from each other, and this made it difficult to enforce municipal justice. Although Cangrejos became independent administratively from Río Piedras in 1773, on several occasions—as in 1823 and 1842—some municipal offices were used by both municipal parties.[1] These circumstances were harmful to the institutional development of Cangrejos and gave rise to an apathy toward authorities by the inhabitants of the district.

A major problem was the lack of sufficient income in the municipal treasury. In 1861, for example, Paul Ubarri wrote to the governor: "I swear

34 | San Mateo de Cangrejos

to Your Excellency that the attached certifies that in the previous month there were no income or expenditures within the municipal funds on behalf of the municipality."[2] How effective could an unstable municipality be without funds to operate? In 1858, the mayor of Cangrejos complained to the governor that he had not received his full pay from the previous year.[3]

The relations between the underpaid mayors and their neighbors, who were reluctant to pay their taxes, were not always cordial. Shortly after the British occupation in 1797, a first lieutenant ironically wrote that in Cangrejos: "Alongside the merits that have allegedly been added to the defense of this Plaza, the residents of Cangrejos Arriba might have added the fine qualities of their clandestine thieves who are stealing cattle in the district as well as in adjacent locales so that on top of having to recover them at home, it aids them in having to drive the stolen cattle, kill them, and distribute them to one and all."[4] Many believe that cattle raids had not started at this time. But even with the mountains, the bad roads, mangroves, and bodies of water in the area, it was still ideal for hiding stolen cattle and fleeing from authority. Ultimately, it was possible to take precautions, as the first lieutenant notes. "Two or three well-bred men who have cattle would introduce themselves to me and ask for license to kill their own cattle in the butcher shop. After granting it, I would find that I had given permission for them to kill cattle, which they and their neighbors had stolen."[5] These criminal associations concerned the municipal magistrate: "At all hours there are hidden in Cangrejos Arriba and aided by its inhabitants . . . delinquents and runaways who settle down in the area with their stolen goods."[6] We tend to believe that all of the inhabitants of the island were neighbors and all white Europeans. We rarely acknowledge that there were also fugitives, thieves, robbers, and criminals, many of whom the authorities were not able to capture: "And they are so skillful and persuasive that even though every night the authorities patrol and record their names in the barracks, it's like a miracle when one of them is imprisoned because once a first lieutenant sergeant major or some official finds one of them, instantly everybody else knows about it and hides in the mountains."[7] This "miracle" demonstrates that there was a relationship between the residents and the criminals against authority. It is therefore not surprising to understand the dynamic noted by the first lieutenant: "To find a crime among such people, even though the judge . . . takes all precautions, you won't even find an infant to tell you the truth about what they've seen and heard."[8] One can speculate that the thieves threatened their neighbors, were related to them, or provided them with money, food, or even safety from the authorities.

No wonder, then, that the authorities began to mingle and unite with those who stole cattle and abducted or seduced women. The first lieutenant himself notes that certain representatives of authority were in league with thieves; they gave them shelter and security against authority:

> The most well-bred man of the said residents is the mayor of the district, and his honor and cunning is such that when I arrived at his house one night there was a self-assured famous cow thief and part-time robber who I had only known by name and this same man, along with those who accompanied me, denied him to me even as he was in my presence and made me note between the number of registered fishermen with a license . . . who were in the home.
>
> This same man kept the Frenchman Pedro Bañe in the home of his brother so that he could send to VS and others who were pursuing him and have not been able to arrest him, and if this happened with the most honest man among these people what can we expect from those without such a good reputation.[9]

Another letter from a member of the Cangrejos authority to the governor reveals an additional feature about surveillance in the district. In 1817, Lieutenant Governor Ignacio Palomares informed the governor that Cangrejos had few city residents who were willing to do jail-guard service, and he warned "that much of the residents have said, that even their children, are unable to do military service, watch service or to help guard prisoners."[10] The total number of participants in the urban militia for that year was 85, including one person who was 14 years old. Palomares pointed out to the governor that "these people have few prisoners sent to the capital from the two East and South shores, they are not hiding them either but guarding these prisoners while they sleep at night in the jail and then taking them to the capital, I have many times seen the extreme

36 | San Mateo de Cangrejos

of them asking for aid . . . from the *Morenos* troop who even though they are paid, are not doing this job because they want to."

Disagreements were also looming in the correspondence among Cangrejos's own authorities. An example could be found in the 1819 official communication of a lieutenant of war who had to ask for two physicians to deal with wounded people: "Yesterday afternoon there were serious injuries to Victorio Coto, a resident of Río Piedras, and to Diego Losada who is from this town and under my jurisdiction." The injured were in serious condition.[11]

The authorities' misgivings about the Black population appears to have been chronic. In another letter it was stated, "Mr. Andres Fuentes . . . the current mayor of the Bridge of San Antonio neighborhood . . . does not have dependable people to go out with him on night patrol, because all the people under his command are Blacks and since he has no friendly relationships with them he does not have the same confidence in them as he would with others."[12]

A gunman, Juan de la Paz Cruz, had a falling out with the mayor of Cangrejos Arriba and reacted angrily: "If I come to find that V. and his son have hurt my cattle I will bash him with a chain." A correspondence grew around this animosity, and the grudges emerged: "Juan de la Paz Cruz' very bad behavior, coupled with that of his children (which is a little worse), has led to the fact that there are daily complaints of theft made against him from his neighbors." It is difficult to gauge the extent of these allegations, but they reveal one way that authority was being exercised and ways authority was being challenged.

For those who have images of a united, happy family that lived in harmony and where peace was the order of the day, let's look at the following: "When Juliana Cortijo accompanied by her mother Petrona Caballero exposed to this government the mistreatment suffered by Juan Mercado, I called them to my presence and it turned out that Juliana had caused friction between Mercado and his wife, leading to disappointments and entanglements."[13] We could add to these instances. But the violence and conflicts could be seen by these testimonies, fragmentations of the famous institutional order of the nineteenth century.

Chapter 8

Cangrejos's Residents:
As Seen from San Juan

Cangrejos's society displays a racial diversity similar to the variety of races that can be found throughout Puerto Rico. In Puerto Rico, as well as in Mexico, "there was a social hierarchy with clear divisions, which affected and prevented upward social mobility." This meant that "one's place in society was determined by race and social class."[1] The strongest proof of how this was shown in society could be found in the categories the census used to classify people. There was a division of the population between Europeans and Spanish Americans; castes, such as mestizos, mulatos, and other ethnically mixed peoples, formed part of the social and racial stratification that was developed in America. Cangrejos and Puerto Rico, were not unique in classifying people like this at the time. "These categories, which were assigned to each individual as they were baptized, referred to their attendant civic and financial qualities even more than to their genetic history."[2] Even though Cangrejos had such residential characteristics, the population of San Mateo de Cangrejos had a low population density; there were few white inhabitants in the district, and the majority of people living there were Black—and most of them were free. It didn't have the merchants to sell its agricultural products, and the district's agriculture was never primarily oriented toward the export market, but only toward supplying food to the island. Ultimately, the strategic importance of Cangrejos helps to round out its main features.

38 | San Mateo de Cangrejos

How did the authorities view Cangrejos's inhabitants? We can try to recreate, with certain facts, the blurry yet revealing picture of Cangrejos.

We begin with an incident that would seem trivial, but it is revealing. In San Juan, there was a growing number of vagrant animals. There was an agreement by the San Juan council in 1775 that said that "Black spear throwers would come from Cangrejos who would kill the dogs, which would give them great satisfaction, at the cost of the city."[3] A few months later, the same problem arose again in the city, and it was suggested that the Blacks of Cangrejos should come and do the work. As we see, it was the type of work that not many people would do, yet the San Juan council believed this was appropriate work for people from Cangrejos:

> In compliance with the agreement designed in accord with the articles of good governance passed by this illustrious City Council, on which there was particular follow-up to the forty-eight, which led to the killing of dogs, pigs and other animals injurious to the common good and of which there was a large excess . . . of dogs . . . so that the spear throwers of Cangrejos come, who enjoy this job.4

Another job for the Cangrejos residents was the repairing of bridges: members of the San Juan Council "agreed to implore the governor, in consideration of his own shortsightedness, to send the Blacks of Cangrejos to cut the stakes which needed cutting, for the neatness, and that they [organize] . . . the terrain so that the passageway to the bridge is safe,"[5] of San Antonio, in 1738.

A more specialized job:

> They created the executioner's office for the death sentences implemented by courts and a Black named Francisco Morin offered to do the job, he was from an English nation, catechized, twenty-five years old, strong body, good height, good color and beardless; they appropriated two silver pesos a month for him and allowed him to live in Hato del Rey, their establishment, and he would come every Sunday to this city with a logo that would be placed on a red cap.[6]

Cangrejos's Residents: As Seen from San Juan | 39

When they needed a place to put those affected by a smallpox epidemic, the council of San Juan, concerned for the residents in the city, had a solution to the problem

> so that we take the important point of caution for the public and the epidemic of smallpox and the methods of protecting those who come out into the square. And to also make temporarily available Mameyes and the County Seat in Cangrejos, as they are windward of the square, this precaution connects with points of San Gerónimo and the San Antonio bridge by their separation from the highway to Río Piedras and by being that intended for those left who were up to now touched by evil.[7]

Who would believe that what is today the major tourist area of Condado was in the past not so remote and instead the place to house the sick and those suffereing from smallpox? The San Juan council was ready to suggest this! "That the county seat building should serve in this respect if by any chance there is an increase in people taken out of the plaza or for convalescence and quarantine and the same for any individual of distinction who has to be forced out."[8]

At the beginning of the nineteenth century, Cangrejos still maintained its tenuous importance. On January 26, 1801, the council "took the present need to promptly establish a legal decree for those with smallpox who have already been affected by this epidemic" and suggested that "Los Mameyes in Cangrejos should be the site for the establishment of the recovery as it would be most advantageous for this effect." Councilor Juan Antonio Mejia was deployed to pass by the site of Los Mameyes "to become acquainted with the hut of Franciso Acosta, and determine if it is in a useable state, and at the same time the county seat building, so that he could report if these locations were convenient."[9] From this information, it can be deduced that there were at least two types of recovery areas, one for the poorest, Los Mameyes, and the county seat building for the more affluent.

It seems that the residents of Cangrejos were not indifferent to these arrangements. In 1804, their complaints were heard by the council: "The hut where the last ones affected by this epidemic have been temporarily

Figure 8.1. Detail of towers and rear of pediment from roof.

placed is very close to Cangrejos' parish church and the neighbors are complaining that they fear being infected."[10]

And yet as late as 1817, there were still records of recovery sites in Cangrejos,[11] even though it does not appear that they were being utilized.

These procedures and agreements by the San Juan Council demonstrate the overall perception of Cangrejos residents in official circles, and it points to how difficult it was for Cangrejos to integrate with the city, even after its annexation in 1862.

Figure 8.2. Detail bell tower, southwest corner.

Chapter 9

Santurce's Urban and Demographic Development

In Puerto Rico, there is a belief that the North American invasion of 1898 helped to civilize us: that it brought knowledge, democracy, and progress. This colonial and distorted idea has been due in part to the kind of history we have been taught. There are areas of the historic discipline that have not been developed—as, for example, local urban historiography, historical demography, and social and economic history. Studies in these areas would help to place 1898 in perspective. This chapter briefly looks at the urban and demographic progress made by the lands annexed in 1862 by San Juan before the invasion by the Americans.

The first thing that should be noted is that in these areas farming was disappearing and that both the population and any urban services of that time began taking over the annexed lands. Ever since the 1860s there was an increase in the establishment of a larger physical infrastructure throughout the area: roads, the central highway (1852), trains (1880), and electric trains (1893). As Zeno confirms, "the urbanization of Santurce continued, slowly and haphazardly at the beginning, but throughout the course of the second half of the 19th century."[1] In 1881, the Jesuit College was built (today this is the location of the Department of Health), and in 1883 the College of Señoritas (mothers) was built.[2] This encouraged people to move to the area, especially along the central highway, which is today Ponce de León Avenue.

42 | San Mateo de Cangrejos

Telephone and train wires went down Ponce de León. "On February 1, 1884," says Marcial Ocasio, "the work to establish a telephone network inside San Juan began . . . However, the line went beyond the capital all the way to Río Piedras."[3] By necessity, it went through Santurce. The modernization of San Juan affected areas around it. In 1892, according to Victor Coll y Cuchi, "San Juan enjoyed a blissful prosperity and the neighborhood of Santurce gentrified quickly. There was an urban railway, a horse-drawn bus train named 'El Bien Publico' and a magnificent luxury car company."[4] In 1890, permission was granted to the municipality of San Juan to create an aqueduct "taking the waters of the Piedras River, dividing it 50 liters per second between Río Piedras, Santurce, and San Juan."[5]

The development of transportation had a particular effect on the transformation of Santurce. Adolfo de Hostos says: "The section of the main highway was opened to traffic . . . and cars began to bring people from the capital to Cangrejos, stimulating the growth of the neighborhood as well."[6] Country houses began to proliferate. Pablo Ubarri received authorization in 1878 to establish a locomotive between San Juan and Río Piedras; his concession would last for 60 years. In 1898, the Puerto Rico Railway Light and Power Company acquired this locomotive; "it immediately stopped running the locomotives and began using the then modern electric cars."[7] Joseph M. Zeno notes that "these easy and economical methods of inter urban transport, established before the automobile was popularized in Puerto Rico, led to a general urbanization of the Santurce district, and, in particular, the formation of the aristocratic 'Condado' neighborhood . . . and the 'Miramar' neighborhood."[8]

The development of the infrastructure coincides with the name change, in 1880, of Cangrejos to Santurce in honor of the noble title of the count of Santurce, which was conceded to Pablo Ubarri for his services to Spain and to Puerto Rico. Ubarri was born in Santurce in the Vizcaya province.[9]

An 1897 description evokes a much more different Santurce than the Cangrejos written about by the chroniclers of the eighteenth century: "The little islet, where the capital rose, joined another larger area, meeting via the San Antonio iron bridge and the locomotive of Ubarri. At the same time, this second islet, where the aristocratic district of Santurce evolved, with its beautiful country houses and showy little hotels, was joined to the big island through the old masonry of the Martín Peña bridge and the live wires of the railway."[10] At the edges of the central highway, the Black population started to be displaced by whites;[11] the rural areas were transformed into urban locations; workplaces became vacation sites. Eventually the tobacco industry also arrived as well as the smelting of iron, and Santurce began to be seen as an appendage to San Juan: "Its streets paved and well populated with modern buildings. Its three large avenues were spacious and full of public buildings of great height. Its theaters, public cafes and recreation sites . . . Everything shows that Santurce is a brand-new, important neighborhood, which completes the great city of San Juan de Puerto Rico."[12] But all this material and technical progress was due to demographic factors and capital projects—such as the investment in transportation. In 1864, the wealth of Cangrejos showed it had 922 residents: among them there were enslaved people, day laborers and property owners. In 1899, 5,840 of San Juan's 32,048 inhabitants lived in the Santurce district. This increased population would need new services and urban facilities.

Conclusion

San Mateo de Cangrejos is a unique case in our national history; it is a district first populated by Black freedmen, fugitives, self-emancipated Blacks, and maroons.

During the course of my investigation, I tried to reconstruct the history of how this town developed, initially in the century when it was first populated. Next, I looked at the chapel, around which the first nucleus of people located themselves, and the importance the church had in the religious life of the inhabitants.

From there, I went on to examine the economic development of Cangrejos during the seventeenth, eighteenth, and nineteenth centuries. The primitive or natural stage of the economy was followed by a farm-based economy, and then eventually an economy based on agriculture, which prevailed until Cangrejos was transformed into the more urban, commercial, and industrial Santurce. It is important to remember the relationship with the market on the island.

Next, I looked at the ethnic origins of the inhabitants in the Cangrejos district. This was basic to an understanding of the importance Blacks have in the cultural and national formation of Puerto Rico and Puerto Ricans. So we see that Blacks were dominant in the area. It's also important to note that slavery was never predominant in the area, and this was not a white neighborhood: dark-skinned, mixed race, and free Blacks were the inhabitants of San Mateo de Cangrejos—these were Black people, of the Caribbean, who were Puerto Rican.

The next item was the review of the strategic location of Cangrejos and its bodies of water for the military defense of the capital. This impor-

46 | San Mateo de Cangrejos

tance was already explicitly noted in the conditions of the area's settlement when it was awarded to Blacks who settled there.

Then I explored the institutional order of Cangrejos according to data found, and then the perceptions about Cangrejos held by the San Juan-based authorities according to the jobs and the responsibilities they created for the district and its inhabitants.

In another chapter I looked at why San Mateo de Cangrejos was taken over: the economic aspect, the territorial needs of the capital, the racial discrimination, and the internal functioning of the municipality. I also highlight the role of Pablo Ubarri as the local mayor from 1864 to 1876.

Finally, I analyzed the urban and demographic development of the area that came to be called Santurce, the noble title it was awarded by Pablo Ubarri in 1880. And it was particularly important to look at the development of city structures and transport from 1880 to 1900.

With these chapters I offer a vision and historical perspective to help us value and understand the role of Black people in our history. Cangrejos still lives in surnames like Cabellero, Andino, Cepeda, Cortijo, Ayala, Andrade, Clemente, Bultrón, Osorio, Castro, Ramos, Escalera, Ferrer, Verdejo, Falú, Llano, Canales, Allende, Vizcarrondo, Pizarrón, Candelaria, Medina, Barriga, Calderón, Escudero, de la O, de la Cruz, de la Rosa, Paris, and Arroyo y Neves. Today you'll find these surnames on the riders, track and field athletes, baseball players, bricklayers, carpenters, electricians, musicians, poets, and boxers. This, then, is their story.

Appendix

Appendix A.1. Origin of the baptized in San Mateo de Cangrejos, 1773–1900

Year	Criollos	Foreigners	Total
1773	10	10	20
1774	28	6	34
1775	24	3	27
1776	21	1	22
1777	23	5	28
1778	26	1	27
1779	18	1	27
1780	26	1	27
1781	28	7	35
1782	21	1	22
1783	38	2	40
1784	26	3	29
1785	32	—	32
1786	30	1	31
1787	29	—	29
1788	34	1	35
1789	32	1	33
1790	32	1	33
1791	25	6	31
1792	27	4	31
1793	32	1	33
1794	34	1	35
1795	33	7	40

continued on next page

48 | Appendix

Appendix A.1. Continued

Year	Criollos	Foreigners	Total
1796	30	1	31
1797	23	1	24
1798	35	1	36
1799	38	1	39
1800	33	—	33
1801	27	1	28
1802	39	2	41
1803	25	—	25
1804	43	—	43

Source: San Mateo de Cangrejos Parish Baptismal Book.

Appendix A.2. Deaths in Cangrejos (1854–1900)

Year	Deaths	Year	Deaths
1854	7	1878	79
1855	46	1879	92
1856	47	1880	122
1857	18	1881	71
1858	44	1882	108
1859	46	1883	75
1860	49	1884	111
1861	49	1885	103
1862	46	1886	88
1863	67	1887	91
1864	76	1888	80
1865	56	1889	88
1866	51	1890	105
1867	38	1891	99
1868	67	1892	111
1869	63	1893	116
1870	70	1894	102
1871	42	1895	107
1872	44	1896	100
1873	37	1897	169
1874	40	1898	157
1875	84	1899	109
1876	93	1900	129
1877	63		

Source: Book of deaths in San Mateo de Cangrejos.

Appendix | 49

Appendix A.3. Population of San Mateo de Cangrejos (1765–1861)

Year	Population	Year	Population
1765	433*	1794	906
1775	436	1795	1280
1776	497	1797	1013
1777	542	1798	1013
1778	555	1799	1384
1779	580	1800	775
1782	573	1801	655
1783	789	1802	859
1784	819	1807	1075*
1785	833	1812	808†
1788	869	1815	842
1789	877	1820	819
1790	955	1824	850‡
1792	860	1828	771§
1793	906	1841	1021**

*Source: Census at the University of Puerto Rico's Center of Historical Investigations.

†AGPR, Spanish Governor's Fund, Series: Census and Wealth, box 12, 13.

‡Manuel Mayoral Barnes, *Historia de Puerto Rico*, page 65.

§Pedro Tomás de Córdoba, Volume II, page 63.

**Center of Historical Investigations, reel 79, bundle 1071, certificate 36.

Appendix A.4a. Ethnic composition of San Mateo de Cangrejos, 1765–1799

	1765	1773	1776	1777	1778	1779	1782	1783	1784	1785	1788	1789	1790	1792	1793	1794	1795	1797	1798	1799
Whites																				
Men			9	7	3			9	9	11	12	11	14	14	9	9	18	26	26	19
Women			6	6	5			6	7	8	10	11	12	12	9	9	12	20	20	8
Boys			6	7	7			9	9	8	13	15	17	16	17	17	22	13	13	9
Girls			4	4	5			16	17	13	9	10	11	11	14	14	31	31	11	9
Free Pardos																				
Men			0	4	4			10	12	10	10	8	6	6	6	6	9	36	36	113
Women			0	5	5			9	9	9	6	5	7	9	7	7	7	15	15	132
Boys			0	6	6			10	11	12	14	15	11	11	11	11	13	24	24	81
Girls			0	7	7			10	13	73	10	14	16	16	16	16	19	13	13	56
Free Morenos																				
Men		43	106	115	233	113	106	151	153	196	167	170	176	176	176	176	216	172	172	200
Women		34	111	112	329	119	109	112	144	147	155	154	160	160	160	160	178	163	163	118
Boys		26	120	115	283	140	128	203	207	212	224	227	233	163	233	233	270	234	234	300
Girls		72	119	129	295	467	111	192	205	207	203	202	213	232	213	213	232	215	215	289
Enslaved Mulatos																				
Men	0	0	1	35	1	2	1	2	1	2	2	3	4	4	4	4	12	6	6	6
Women	0	2	29	2	3	2	1	2	1	2	1	2	2	2	2	2	30	5	5	1
Boys	0	0	0	4	0	0	0	0	0	0	0	1	0	0	0	0	19	2	2	6
Girls	0	0	0	0	0	0	0	0	0	0	0	0	1	0	0	0	21	3	3	2

Appendixes | 51

Enslaved Blacks																			
Whites																			
Free Pardos	7	9	16	250	14	19	14	13	14	15	14	10	10	17	17	52	18	18	7
Free Morenos	4	9	6	402	4	3	5	7	8	10	10	6	6	12	12	35	16	16	16
Enslaved Mulatos	0	0	0	0	0	0	0	0	0	0	0	7	0	0	0	19	13	13	9
Enslaved Blacks	0	0	0	0	0	0	0	0	0	0	6	6	0	0	20	8	8	8	4
Aggregate Total																			
General Overview																			
Whites	141	29	24	22	17	16	40	42	40	44	47	54	54	49	49	83	70	70	44
Free Blacks	220		22	22	20	20	39	45	44	46	42	40	40	40	40	48	88	88	382
Enslaved Mulatos	23		471	483	529	454	688	709	722	751	760	782	782	931	782	836	784	784	907
Enslaved Blacks	49	77	2	25	18	19	20	22	23	24	20	29	29	29	29	126	55	55	36
Total	433	436	497	542	553	580	573	789	819	833	869	877	955	860	906	1280	1013	1013	1384

Source: Census at the University of Puerto Rico's Center of Historical Investigations.

52 | San Mateo de Cangrejos

Appendix A.4b. Ethnic composition of San Mateo de Cangrejos, 1800–1861

	1800	1801	1802	1807	1812	1815	1820	1824	1828	1841	1842	1856	1861
Whites													
Men	30	20	25	30	13	13	11			13	8	48	81
Women	18	15	27	23	14	14	11			13	11	31	49
Boys	24	24	28	27	26	26	6			33	20		
Girls	12	20	27	32	16	16	9			17	22		
Free Pardos													
Men	11	18	15	20	76	108	100			114	116	499	646
Women	9	15	12	13	94	110	120			108	106	578	704
Boys	2	24	12	14	156	80	170			209	222		
Girls	3	18	7	12	124	73	170			208	219		
Free Morenos													
Men	106	75	100	200	23	45	9			16	15	88	84
Women	124	87	126	140	24	54	17			13	14	94	90
Boys	163	133	181	208	38	110	7			37	40		
Girls	163	137	198	213	42	115	11			26	44		
Enslaved Mulatos													
Men	3	1	3	4						10	10	38	70
Women	5	0	1	3						10	11	20	7
Boys	1	0	3	5						106	95		
Girls	0	0	2	6						88	82		

Enslaved Blacks													
Men	58	45	71	75	93	1			22	76	61		6
Women	20	14	18	28	16	4			27	639	663		6
Boys	10	4	6	12		13			582	92	113		
Girls	13	1	3	10		8							
General Overview													
Whites	84	79	101	112	69	69	37						130
Free Pardos	25	75	46	59	450	371	580						1353
Free Morenos	556	432	605	761	127	324	44						174
Enslaved							115						
Mulatos	9	1	9	18	99	26	43		114	214	198		77
Enslaved													
Blacks	101	64	86	125	63	52	819		26				12
Aggregate Total	775	655	859	1075	808	842		850	771	1021	1035	1396	1746

Source: Census at the University of Puerto Rico's Center of Historical Investigations.

54 | Appendix

Appendix A.5. Population structure by age in San Mateo de Cangrejos: 1765 and 1841

Cangrejos and Rio Piedras

1765	Men	Women	Total
Up to 10 years	86	81	167
10 to 15 years	70	60	130
15 to 40 years	153	175	328
40 to 60 years	70	45	115
60 years old and older	29	23	52
Totals	408	384	792*

Cangrejos

1841	
1 to 10 years	316
11 to 20 years	191
21 to 30 years	330
31 to 40 years	116
41 to 50 years	70
51 to 60 years	51
61 to 70 years	22
71 to 80 years	5
81 to 90 years	3
91 to 100 years	7
101 to 110 years	1†

*Source: Aida R. Caro, *Antologia de historia de Puerto Rico*, 399.

†Source: Center of Historical Investigations, reel 79, bundle 1071, certificate 36, 1841.

Appendix A.6. Known Authorities in Cangrejos between 1773 and 1876

Name	Title	Dates
Pedro Cortijo	Military Captain	1773[1]
Ignacio Palomares		1817[2]
Jaime Kiernan	Mayor	1818
Antonio Dalmán	Mayor	1820
Don Eusebio Noa	Mayor	1826
Francisco Enciso	War Lieutenant	1832
Gaspar Bilas	Presiding mayor of Rio Piedras and Cangrejos	1838
Miguel Campanor	Municipal Mayor of Rio Piedras and Cangrejos	1844
Antonio Román	Mayor of Rio Piedras and Cangrejos	1846
Fontat de Aldrey	War Lieutenant of Rio Piedras and Cangrejos	1849
Ramón Ramos	Cangrejos Mayor	1856
Mardon Hardoy	Accidental Mayor	1859
[Mardon?] Hardoy	Ordinary Mayor	1859
[Ramón?] Ramos	Ordinary Mayor	1859
Rafael Villafañe	Mayor	1861
Pablo Ubarri	Accidental Mayor[3]	1861
Pablo Ubarri	Representative Mayor	1864–1876

[1] The year when Governor Muesas allowed Cangrejos to become an independent municipality, and when Pedro Cortijo and 55 other blacks petitioned the governor for it (1770–1776). There was a period when Cangrejos belonged to Rio Piedras administratively, and did not have autonomy.

[2] We do not know who the party's officials were during the 18th century, up to 1817. We also do not know who the officials of San Mateo de Cangrejos were during the 17th century.

[3] Don Pablo Ubarri, became the most powerful political figure in the latter half of the 19th century. And it is precisely due to Cangrejos that Pablo Ubarri wa able to have his base of political and economic power on the island. Once San Mateo was suppressed in 1862, Don Pablo Ubarri, occupied the mayor's office, where a struggle arose between two powers: the municipality and Cangrejos.

Source: General Archive of Puerto Rico. San Juan City Hall.

56 | Appendix

Appendix A.7. Important dates and events in San Mateo de Cangrejos

Date	Event
1613	Mention of Cangrejos: (catalog of the letters and petitions of the Cabildo of San Juan Bautista of Puerto Rico in the Archivo General de Indias) (16–18 centuries).
seventeenth century	Fugitives from non-Spanish territories establish the town of Cangrejos. These fugitives were of African descent: they were the former slaves and Africans. These first inhabitants originally settled in Puerta de Tierra, and from there they moved on to settle near the cano of San Antonio.
1729	Bishop Sebastian Lorenzo makes it known that he has established Cangrejo's Chapel.
1760	Construction begins on the church of San Mateo de Cangrejos but not of the foundation of the village, which dates back to the seventeenth century.
1773	Upon the urging of Pedro Cortijo and some 55 Black Cangrejans, Governor Muesas grants Cortijo independent authority over Cangrejos. Governor Muesas separates the district of Cangrejos from Rio Piedras; the military is under the jurisdiction of Rio Piedras, the church is in Bayamon, and the Royal Property is in the capital.
1797	The British attack and occupy Cangrejos and remain on the island for several weeks. Cangrejos had previously been attacked by both English and French invading forces.
1862	The village of Cangrejos is expunged and annexed to form part of San Juan, Carolina, and the Rio Piedras territory. The role of auxiliary mayor is also created at this time, a position occupied by Pablo Ubarri until 1876, when he was removed.
1876	The role of Auxiliary Mayor—which is occupied by Pablo Ubarri—is removed.
1880	The name of Cangrejos is changed to Santurce based on the noble titled bestowed on Pablo Ubarri by the Spanish Crown.

Source: General Archive of Puerto Rico. San Juan City Hall.

Glossary

Cédula is a license, decree, official document, or certificate issued by the government.

Cédula de Gracias or Real Cédula de Gracias (Royal Decree of Graces)—a decree that granted Puerto Rico greater economic freedom. Published under the government of Felipe VII on August 10, 1815, the Cédula was designed to foster new tax changes, free trade, and a more liberal immigration policy among Spain's colonies.

Moreno, mulatto, grifo, pardo, zambo, and mestizo are racial classifications pointing to the degree of African heritage a person of color is reported to have. *Moreno* literally means brown; *mulatto* is the offspring of a Black person and a white person; *grifo* refers to a person with light or white skin and kinky hair (it is from the Latin *gryphus* which means "twisted"); *pardo* denotes a person who has some mix of European, Amerindian, and/or African ancestry; *zambo* is the offspring of an African and an indigenous person; and *mestizo* means light-skinned *mulatto*.

Real Compañía de Comercio para los islas dé Santo Domingo, Puerto Rico y La Margarita or Real Compañía is Spain's Royal Company representing the business interests of shareholders in Spain.

Reales or *reales de plata* (silver coins) was the name for Spanish currency up until the mid-1800s. Reales were used in Spain and throughout its colonies.

Notes

Introduction

1. *San Mateo de Cangrejos: Historical Notes on a Self-Liberated Black Community in Puerto Rico* was originally published as *San Mateo de Cangrejos, comunidad cimarrona en Puerto Rico: Notas para su historia* by Gilberto Aponte Torres. The book was first published in 1985 by the San Juan, Puerto Rico–based Comité de Historia de los Pueblos).

2. Elinor Des Verney Sinnette, *Arthur Alfonso Schomburg: Black Bibliophile and Collector* (New York Public Library and Wayne State UP, 1989).

3. Vanessa K. Valdés, *Diasporic Blackness: The Life and Times of Arturo Alfonso Schomburg* (SUNY Press, 2017).

4. Evelyne Laurent-Perrault, "Arturo Alfonso Schomburg, the Quintessential Maroon: Toward an African Diasporic Epistemology," *small axe* 61 (2020): 132–41.

5. Arthur A. Schomburg, "The Negro Digs Up His Past," in *The New Negro*, ed. Alain Locke (1925, Atheneum, 1992), 231–37.

Chapter 1

1. See José Joaquín Real Díaz, *Catalogue of Letters and Petitions of the Town Council of San Juan Bautista of Puerto Rico in the General Archives of the Indies* ([Catálogo de las cartas y peticiones del cabildo de San Juan Bautista de Puerto Rico en el Archivo General de Indias, siglos 16–18. Recopilación y notas por José J. Real Díaz] San Juan, 1968). "Accompanying: Copy of the testimonial of Francisco de Negrete's town council, requesting by letter that the governor of the island appoint a mayor with jurisdiction over the area from the banks of Bayamón, Toa, and Luisa and the towns of Arecibo, Manati, Coamo, Pueblo Viejo, Cangrejos, etc., in view of the frequent crimes and robberies that are committed" (Act

176, 1613, 145). Although this record has been sought in the Historical Research Center at Docket 165, reel number 49, it has not been found. There may be an error in the synopsis of the document. Either way, there are other data sources that pose the origins of Cangrejos in the seventeenth century.

2. Salvador Brau, *The Colonization of Puerto Rico* ((La colonización de Puerto Rico) 2nd edition (San Juan: 1969), 364.

3. Maria de los Angeles Castro, "Urban and architectural values/ Valores urbanos y arquitectonicos," *Cuadernos de la Facultad de Humanidades* 3 (1979): 11.

4. Ibid., 12.

5. According to Cayetano Coll y Toste, Don Juan Perez de Guzman, Field Master, who took office on August 16, 1660, and ruled until December 1664, protected the fugitive enslaved people from the Danish island of Saint Croix, who had fled to Puerto Rico to escape their masters. Island authorities and royal decrees prohibited these fugitives from being re-enslaved.

6. Frederico Ribes Tovar, *Chronological History of Puerto Rico/Historia cronologica de Puerto Rico* (San Juan, 1973), 116.

7. Paul G. Miller, *History of Puerto Rico/Historia de Puerto Rico* (San Juan, 1949), 202.

8. Ibid., 203.

9. Ibid.

10. Adolfo de Hostos, *Historia de San Juan, Ciudad Murada* [History of San Juan: The Walled City] (San Juan, 1966), 83.

11. José Colomban Rosario y Justina Carrión, *El negro: Haiti, Estados Unidos* [Blacks: of Haiti, the United States, and Puerto Rico] (Universidad de Puerto Rico, Division de Impresos, 1951), p. 106. https://books.google.com/books/about/El_negro.html?id=h6LaOwAACAAJ.

12. Cayetano Coll y Toste, *Boletin Histórico de Puerto Rico I*, 16.

13. Alejandro Tapia y Rivera, *Biblioteca histórica de Puerto Rico III*, 604–5.

14. Cayetano Coll y Toste, *Boletin Histórico de Puerto Rico I*, 26.

15. Manuel Barnes Mayoral, *Historia de Puerto Rico I*, 63.

16. Guillermo Baralt, *Rebel Slaves/Esclavos rebeldes* (Río Piedras, 1982), 24.

17. Ibid.

Chapter 2

1. Jorge David Díaz, "Estudio sobre el clero de Caguas en el siglos XIX" ["Study on the clergy of Caguas in the nineteenth century"]. https://revistas.upr.edu/index.php/ch/article/view/8723

2. Ibid., 74–75.

3. Paul G. Miller, *Historia de Puerto Rico* (New York: Rand McNally, 1922), p. 200. https://www.loc.gov/item/22023871/.

4. Luis M. Díaz Soler, *Historia de la esclavitud negra en Puerto Rico* (History of Black slavery in Puerto Rico) (Río Piedras), 235–36.

Chapter 3

1. See Iñigo Abbad y Lasierra and José J Acosta, *Historia geográfica, civil y natural de la isla de San Juan Bautista de Puerto-Rico [Geographic, civil and natural history of the island of San Juan Bautista de Puerto Rico]*, p. 119. Puerto-Rico, Impr. y librería de Acosta, 1866. Pdf. https://www.loc.gov/item/03006061/.

2. André-Pierre Ledrü, *Viaje a la Isla de Puerto Rico*, translated to Spanish by J. L. Vizcarrondo II, ed. (Río Piedras, 1957).

3. *Proceedings of the San Juan Town Council*, 1730–1750, 73.

4. *Proceedings of the San Juan Town Council*, 1774–1777, 233–34.

5. *Proceedings of the San Juan Town Council*, 1777–1781, 7.

6. Ibid., 129.

7. *Proceedings of the San Juan Town Council*, 1792–1799, 205.

8. *Proceedings of the San Juan Town Council*, 1751–1760, 85.

9. *Proceedings of the San Juan Town Council*, 1781–1785, 68.

10. *Proceedings of the San Juan Town Council*, 1774–1777, 71–72.

11. *Proceedings of the San Juan Town Council*, 1792–1799, 37.

12. *Proceedings of the San Juan Town Council*, 1751–1760, 169.

13. Ibid.

14. Aida R. Caro Costas, ed., *Antologia de lecturas de historia de Puerto Rico* [Anthology of lectures on the history of Puerto Rico] (Río Piedras, Puerto Rico: 1983), 400.

15. Ibid., 549.

16. AGPR, Fondo de Gobernadores Espanoles de Puerto Rico, Censo y Riqueza. [Spanish Governor's Fund of Puerto Rico, Census and Wealth], box 13, unnumbered file production reports, 1812.

17. Ibid., box 11. "Cangrejos district . . . 1818."

18. Ibid.

19. Ibid., Cities. Cangrejos, box 429.

20. AGPR, Archivo General de Puerto Rico (General Archives of Puerto Rico), military affairs, box 261, records of Cangrejos.

Chapter 4

1. See Eugenio Fernández Méndez, *Crónicas de Puerto Rico*, 303.
2. Miller, 288.
3. Díaz Soler, 395.

Chapter 5

1. Íñigo Abbad, 119.
2. *Boletin de Historia de Puerto Rico*, 6, 384.
3. Bibiano Torres Ramirez, *La isla de Puerto Rico* (1765–1800), 17
4. Íñigo Abbad, 220.
5. Aida Caro Costas, *Antologia de lecturas de historia de Puerto Rico*, 461.
6. Britain's lieutenant general, Sir Ralph Abercromby, invaded Puerto Rico in April 1797.
7. Bibiano Torres Ramirez, *La isla de Puerto Rico* (1765–1800), 17.
8. Caro, *Antologia*, 462.
9. André-Pierre Ledrú, 127.
10. *Boletin de Historia de Puerto Rico*, 7, 260.
11. Sevilla, Archivo General de Indias, legajo 2522; consulted on microfiche in the Historical Investigations center.
12. Ibid.
13. Angel Rivero, *Cronica de la Guerra Hispanoamericana en Puerto Rico*, 55.

Chapter 6

1. Archivo General de Puerto Rico (General Archives of Puerto Rico). Year: 1875, v. 57, exp. 49.
2. Ibid.
3. Ibid.
4. AGPR, Public Works, Public Property, box 34, Carolina, 1864.
5. Ibid., 1876.
6. Ibid., box 195, Río Piedras, 1829.
7. Ibid., 1806.
8. AGPR. Council Fund of San Juan, leg. 57, exp. 22, 1864.
9. Ibid., box 147, leg. 5, 1860.
10. Ibid.

Notes to Chapter 8 | 63

11. Ibid., leg. 57, exp. 22.
12. De Hostos, *Historia de San Juan, Ciudad Murada*, 88.
13. AGPR San Juan Town Hall, leg. 4, exp. 143, 1876.
14. Ibid.
15. Ibid.
16. Ibid., leg. 3, exp. 129, 1876.

Chapter 7

1. See FGEPR, box 429, "Dossier on the restoration of San Mateo and the legitimacy of their rights. "
2. Ibid., letter from 1861.
3. Ibid., letter from 1858.
4. AGPR, Obras Publicas, Propiedad Publica [Public Works, Public Property], Carolina, box 32, 1804.
5. Ibid.
6. Ibid.
7. Ibid.
8. Ibid.
9. Ibid.
10. FGEPR, Cangrejos, box 429, office of the governor.
11. Ibid., official correspondence of 1819.
12. Ibid., Río Piedras, box 544
13. Ibid., Cangrejos, box 429.

Chapter 8

1. D. A. Brading, *Mineros y comerciantes en el Mexico borbonico* (1763–1810), 39–40.
2. Ibid.
3. Actas del Caibildo de San Juan, January 30, 1775, 99.
4. Ibid., April 3, 1775, 114.
5. Ibid., October 22, 1738, 145.
6. Ibid., June 19, 1764, 69.
7. Ibid., June 21, 1801, 242.
8. Ibid., June 26, 1801, 243–44.
9. Ibid., December 5, 1803, 22–23.

64 | Notes to Chapter 9

10. Ibid., June 11, 1804, 77–78.

11. Ibid., January 13, 1817, 214.

Chapter 9

1. J. M. Zeno, *Historia de la capital de Puerto Rico* [History of Puerto Rico's capital], 90.

2. Various authors, *Lealtad y heroism de la Isla de Puerto Rico* [Loyalty and Heroism on the island of Puerto Rico], 330.

3. Marcial E. Ocasio Meléndez, *El desarrollo urbano de Río Piedras (1868–1899)* [The urban development of Río Piedras (1868–1899)], master's thesis in history, Universidad de Puerto Rico, 140.

4. Victor Coll y Cuchi, *Estampas Puertorriquenas* [Portraits of Puerto Rico], 59–60.

5. Ibid., p. 58.

6. Adolfo de Hostos, *Crecimiento y desarrollo de la ciudad de San Juan* [Growth and development of the city of San Juan], 22–23.

7. Map of the city and neighborhoods of San Juan, 8.

8. José M. Zeno, *Historia de la Capital de Puerto Rico* [History of the capital of Puerto Rico], 91.

9. Leandro Fanjul González, *Don Pablo Ubarri y Puerto Rico*, master's thesis in history, Universidad de Puerto Rico, 5.

10. Various authors, *Lealtad y heroism de la Isla de Puerto Rico*, master's thesis in history, 330.

11. Adolfo de Hostos, *Diccionario historico*, 216.

12. Victor Coll y Cuchi, 63.

Bibliographies

Original Bibliography

Abbad y Lasierra, Iñigo and José J Acosta. *Historia geográfica, civil y natural de la isla de San Juan Bautista de Puerto-Rico [Geographic, civil and natural history of the island of San Juan Bautista de Puerto Rico].* Puerto-Rico, Impr. y librería de Acosta, 1866. Pdf. https://www.loc.gov/item/03006061/.

Coll y Cuchi, Victor. Estampas Puertorriquenas [Portraits of Puerto Rico]. Puerto Rio Departamento de Instruccion publica, 1964.

Díaz, Jorge David. 1979. "Estudio sobre el clero de Caguas: Siglo XIX". Universidad de Puerto Rico Cuadernos de la Facultad de Humanidades 3:67-138. http://smjegupr.net/newsite/wp-content/uploads/2020/02/Estudio-sobre-el-clero-de-caguas-siglo-XIX-por-Jorge-David-D-az.pdf.

Miller, Paul G. *Historia de Puerto Rico.* New York: Rand McNally, 1922. https://www.loc.gov/item/22023871/.

Tapia y Rivera, Alejandro. *Biblioteca historica de Puerto Rico.* Volume III. San Juan: Instituto de Cultura Puertorriquena, 1970.

Todd, Roberto H. *Estampas coloniales.* San Juan: Imprenta Venezuela, 1946.

Torres Ramirez, Bibiano. *La isla de Puerto Rico (1763–1880).* San Juan: Instituto de Cultura Puertorriquena, 1968.

Ubeda y Delgado, Manuel. *Isla de Puerto Rico.* San Juan: Establecimiento Tip. Del Boletin, 1878.

Various authors. *Lealtad y heroismo de la isla de Puerto Rico.* San Juan: Imprenta de A. Lyn e hijos de Perez Moris, 1897.

Zeno, José M. *Historia de la Capital de Puerto Rico.* San Juan: Publicacion Oficial del Gobierno de la Capital, 1959.

Updated Bibliography

Baralt, Guillermo A., translated by Christine Ayorinde. *Slave Revolts in Puerto Rico: Conspiracies and Uprisings, 1795–1873*. Princeton, NJ: Markus Wiener Publishers, 2007.

Negron Portillo, Mariano and Raul Mayo Santana. *La esclavitud menor: la esclavitud en los municipios del interior de Puerto Rico en el siglo XIX*. San Juan: Centro de Investigaciones Sociales, UPR, 2007.

Picó, Fernando. *History of Puerto Rico: A Panorama of Its People*. Princeton, NJ: Markus Wiener Publishers, 2006.

Sepúlveda, Aníbal, and Jorge Carbonell. *San Juan Extramuros: Iconografía para su estudio*. San Juan: Centro de Investigaciones CARIMAR/Oficina Estatal de Preservación Histórica, 1990.

Ungerleider Kepler, David. *Fiestas Santiago Apóstol Loíza: La cultura Afro Puertorriqueña ante los procesos de hibridación y globalización*. San Juan: Isla Negra Editores, 2000.

Index

Abad, Iñigo, 7, 25–26
Abercromby, Ralph, 26
Africans
  counting number of, 6–8
  emancipated, 4–5, 9, 27
  enslaved, 4, 6–7
  migrant movement, 4
  offering land to, 4–5
  self-liberated, 6–7
agrofishing production, importance of, 15–16
animals, economic activity, 19
Aruz, José, 28

Baralt, Guillermo, 7
Bayamón, 26
Blacks, 3, 23–24
  and institutional order, 34–36
  and military defense, 25–26
  as residents, 37–40
  self-emancipated, 5, 7, 25, 45
Bridge (Parada 26 and Barrio Obrero), 10
Britain, 26, 34

Caballero, Petrona, 36
Calderon, Bernardo, 11
Canales, Domingo, 12

Cangrejos Arriba, borough, 1–2, 10, 12, 16, 28, 34, 36
  heads of households in, 17
  municipal income for public expenditures in, 17
  subsidy payments in, 18
  wealth in, 20
Carolina, 27
cedula, 4
Cédula de Gracias, 7
chapel, placement of, 9–10
chickens, 19
Church of San Mateo, 10
church, San Mateo de Cangrejos, 9–10
  early economic activities, 9
  integrating Caribbean Black, 10
  original urban center, 9
  placement of chapels, 9–10
College of Señoritas, 41
colonies, 6
Coto, Victorio, 36
cows, 14–15, 19
Cuchi, Victor Coll y, 42
Cuerda, Francisco de la, 26
cultivated land, value of, 18

Díaz, Jorge David, 9
district, 1–2

68 | Index

donkey, 14–15, 19

economic activity, San Mateo de
Cangrejos
agrofishing production, 16
animals, 19
census report, 14
city supplies, 11–12
cultivated land, 18
fishing industry, 11–13
foodstuffs, 11
heads of households, 17
land tenure, 20–21
livestock quotas, 13
municipal property wealth, 15
municipal income for public
expenditures, 16–17
overcoming primitive economy,
13–14
plantings, 14–15
sources of wealth, 19–20
subsidy payments, 17–18
total values, 15
wealth by neighborhood, 16–21
wealth in, 19–20
ethnic origins, San Mateo de
Cangrejos, 23–24

fishing, economic activity, 11–13
foodstuffs, 11

González, Fernando Miyares, 24
grifo, 24
Guaynabo, 26

Hato del Rey, borough, 10, 16
heads of households in, 17
municipal income for public
expenditures in, 17
subsidy payments in, 18
wealth in, 20

Hato Rey, 1
horses, 14–15, 19
households, number of heads of, 16–
17

immigration, encouraging, 4–5
institutional order, San Mateo de
Cangrejos, 33–36
Isla Verde, 1

Jesuit College, 41
Justina, José Colombán Rosario y, 6

land, offering, 5
Ledru, Andre-Pierre, 11
livestock, 13
Los Mameyes, 39
Losada, Diego, 36

Machuchal, borough, 10, 16
heads of households in, 17
municipal income for public
expenditures in, 17
subsidy payments in, 18
wealth in, 20
mares, 15, 19
Martín Peña canal/stream, 6, 11–12,
25–26
mayor-neighbor relations, 34–35
Mercado, Juan, 36
mestizo, 24, 37
military defense, San Mateo de
Cangrejos, 25–26
modernization, San Mateo de
Cangrejos, 41–43
morenos, 24, 25, 36
Muesas, Miguel de, 10
mulato, 24, 37
mules, 14–15, 19
municipal boundary. *See* district
Muriel, Ignacio, 11

Noa, Eusebio, 15

origins, San Mateo de Cangrejos, 3–8
   African migrant movement, 4
   number of refugees, 6–8
   observing historical development, 3–4
   size of urban core, 4
oxen, 14–15, 19

Palomares, Ignacio, 35
passages, leases of, 12
Paz Cruz, Juan de la, 36
pigs, 1, 14–15, 39
Pizarro, Sebastian Lorenzo, 10
Pizzaro, Don, 12
plantings, 14–15
Ponce de León Avenue, 41–42
public expenditure, municipal income for, 16–17
Puente, borough, 16
   heads of households in, 17
   municipal income for public expenditures in, 17
   subsidy payments in, 18
   wealth in, 20
Puerta de Tierra, 5
Puerto de Tierra, 3
Puerto Rico, 3–4, 37. See also San Mateo de Cangrejos (Cangrejos)
   early economic activities in, 9
   Santurce urbanization, 41–43

racial categories, 23–24
residents, San Mateo de Cangrejos, 37–40
Río Piedras, 1, 10, 25, 26, 27, 33
river estuaries, leases of, 13
Robe, El, 7
Rodríguez, Victoriano, 28

San Antonio canal, 6, 11–12
San Juan, 1, 27
   and suppression, 27–31
   town council, 13–14, 38–39
San Mateo de Cangrejos (Cangrejos), 1–2, 45–46
   church of, 9–10
   economic activity in, 11–21
   ethnic origins of, 23–24
   institutional order of, 33–36
   military defense, 25–26
   modernization of, 41–43
   origins of, 3–8
   residents, 37–40
   Santurce urbanization, 41–43
   suppression in, 27–31
Santana, Andrés de, 12
Santurce, urbanization in, 1, 41–43
Seboruco, borough, 10, 16, 26
   heads of households in, 17
   municipal income for public expenditures in, 17
   subsidy payments in, 18
   wealth in, 20
Seboruco, name, 9
settlements
   terms referring to, 9
   and wealth, 16–21
smallpox, 39
"State of the Island of Puerto Rico," census, 23
subsidy payments, 17–18
suppression, San Mateo de Cangrejos, 27–31
   access to land, 28
   annexation, 28
   factors, 27–28
   fiscal issues, 28–29
   racial prejudices, 28–29
   Royal Order of November 11, 1862, 29

70 | Index

transportation, development of, 42
turkeys, 19

Ubarri, Pablo, 29–31, 33–34, 42

Vacia Talega lagoon, 25

wealth, sources of, 19–20
whites, 23–24

zambo, 24
Zengotita, Juan Bautista de, 26
Zeno, Joseph M., 41